The
Best-Kept
Teaching
Secret

With special thanks to

Michele Timble, Burley Elementary School, Chicago, IL

Debbie King, Burley Elementary School, Chicago, IL

Sara Ahmed, The Bishop's School, La Jolla, CA

Kristin Ziemke, Burley Elementary School, Chicago, IL

Brad Buhrow, Columbine Elementary School, Boulder, CO

Michelle Nash, Burley Elementary School, Chicago, IL

Nancy Steineke, Andrew High School, Tinley Park, IL

Sheridan High School, Sheridan, AR

Federal Hocking Local Schools, Stewart, OH

Disney II Magnet School, Chicago, IL

Smokey & Elaine

Harvey "Smokey" Daniels & Elaine Daniels

The Best-Kept Teaching Secret

How Written Conversations Engage Kids, Activate Learning, and Grow Fluent Writers, K–12

CL CORWIN LITERACY

CORWIN
A SAGE Company

FOR INFORMATION:

Corwin
A SAGE Company
2455 Teller Road
Thousand Oaks, California 91320
(800) 233-9936
www.corwin.com

SAGE Publications Ltd.
1 Oliver's Yard
55 City Road
London EC1Y 1SP
United Kingdom

SAGE Publications India Pvt. Ltd.
B 1/I 1 Mohan Cooperative Industrial Area
Mathura Road, New Delhi 110 044
India

SAGE Publications Asia-Pacific Pte. Ltd.
3 Church Street
#10-04 Samsung Hub
Singapore 049483

Publisher: Lisa Luedeke
Development Editor: Julie Nemer
Editorial Assistant: Francesca Dutra Africano
Production Editor: Melanie Birdsall
Copy Editor: Melinda Masson
Typesetter: C&M Digitals (P) Ltd.
Proofreader: Wendy Jo Dymond
Indexer: Sheila Bodell
Cover Designer: Rose Storey

Copyright © 2013 by Corwin

Photo credits for chapter-opening photos:
Chapter 1: Copyright © Rhoda Sidney/PhotoEdit. All rights reserved.
Chapter 2: Copyright © Spencer Grant/PhotoEdit. All rights reserved.
Chapter 3: Copyright © Michael Newman/PhotoEdit. All rights reserved.
Chapter 4: Copyright © David Young-Wolff/PhotoEdit. All rights reserved.
Chapter 5: Copyright © James Shaffer/PhotoEdit. All rights reserved.
Chapter 6: Copyright © Jim West/PhotoEdit. All rights reserved.

Printed in the United States of America

Library of Congress Cataloging-in-Publication Data

Daniels, Harvey.
The best-kept teaching secret : how written conversations engage kids, activate learning, and grow fluent writers, K–12 / Harvey "Smokey" Daniels, Elaine Daniels.
pages cm
Includes bibliographical references and index.
ISBN 978-1-4522-6863-7 (pbk.)

1. English language—Composition and exercises—Study and teaching (Elementary) 2. Letter writing—Study and teaching (Elementary) 3. Communication in education. 4. Active learning. I. Daniels, Elaine. II. Title.

LB1576.D232 2013
372.62'3—dc23   2013021342

This book is printed on acid-free paper.

SUSTAINABLE FORESTRY INITIATIVE
Certified Chain of Custody
Promoting Sustainable Forestry
www.sfiprogram.org
SFI-01268
SFI label applies to text stock

13 14 15 16 17 10 9 8 7 6 5 4 3 2 1

Contents

Contents

Contents

Contents

Click on Smokey and Elaine's book at
www.corwin.com/literacy
and navigate to the "Supplements" tab
to view downloadable resources.

Acknowledgments

After 38 years of marriage and countless years of teaching, we have finally written our first book together. Why did we wait so long, given that Smokey has written 18 books in the interim? Well, we wanted to be sure the relationship would survive the perils of co-authorship. Raising kids and building a family seemed like minor dangers compared to the marital risks entailed in writing a book with a spouse. But now, the manuscript is complete, and no legal papers have been served, so we guess it worked. We should have started sooner!

Without a jumbo posse of co-conspirators, this book would not have been possible. We have been working on this, our fondest project, for more than 20 years. During that time, we developed this book's strategies in our own classrooms, where, between us, we have now taught every grade from kindergarten through college, at least as guests, if not employees.

And during all that time we've also been collaborating with a big, loose network of teacher-pioneers all around the county. We've been connected by our belief that written conversation is the single most neglected tool in our teaching repertoires—and that developing many examples and sharing them with colleagues is an entirely delicious pursuit. So above all, we thank all the teachers who tried our ideas with their kids, invited us into their classrooms, told us their teaching stories, and gave us many samples of kids' work that are the core of the book.

It has been a joy to get to work with the energetic and talented Corwin crew, as they launch a brand-new line of professional books on literacy. The moment that our longtime colleague and friend Lisa Luedeke was hired to build this unique list, we voted "in." Then, when marketing maven Maura Sullivan signed on, we knew the book would find its audience. And now that we have gotten to know Editorial Director Lisa Shaw and CEO Mike Soules, we know we are joining a team with a vision for the future of teaching firmly in mind.

Thanks to everyone who makes our work such a pleasure.

—Smokey and Elaine Daniels
Santa Fe, New Mexico

Letters Leverage
Learning

Dear Colleagues,

*We are Smokey and Elaine Daniels, a couple of longtime
teachers. We have taught kids of all ages, and in many
regions of the United States, for more decades than we
care to admit. And right now, we want to share our single
best teaching strategy with you.*

Smokey and Elaine

This book is about a close-knit family of teaching and learning structures that changed our classrooms in very big ways. In fact, this is *the single most important teaching idea we have ever learned.* And we use it *every single school day* to structure powerful interactions among our students.

The core idea here is *written conversation*—a wide variety of letter types including handwritten notes, emails, dialogue journals, write-arounds, silent literature circles, collaborative annotation, threaded discussions, blogs, text messages, tweets, and more. We use these special writing activities to conduct a huge range of learning activities with our students. Year in and year out, the kids tell us this is one of their favorite ways to work, think, and interact with each other.

We know what you're thinking: "Hmmm, this sounds like a kind of small idea." Everyone thinks that before they try it. But we're going to prove to you that letters—very broadly defined—are the single most neglected tool in our teaching repertoires. Here are some benefits this powerful genre of writing offers for your classroom.

BENEFITS OF WRITTEN CONVERSATIONS

- Replace sleepy whole-class lectures with thoughtful, lively interaction
- Enable active, engaged learning and knowledge-building in all subjects
- Create vigorous discussion of curricular ideas and concepts
- Provide effective differentiation in today's diverse classrooms
- Build fluency, confidence, and a positive attitude toward writing
- Give kids practice in narrative, explanatory, and argumentative writing
- Teach kids to ask follow-up questions
- Teach kids to back up their thinking with evidence
- Provide opportunities for one-to-one coaching, guidance, and feedback
- Gather rich, concrete data for formative and formal assessment

- Create a climate of collaboration, community, high morale, and productivity
- Offer models of great writing styles and effective composing strategies
- Empower kids to make good decisions and take responsibility
- Motivate reluctant students
- Give shy and reticent students a safe way to go public and shine
- Provide a natural opportunity for English language learners to excel
- Minimize classroom management problems
- Push kids' thinking
- Enlist students as extra teachers in your classroom
- Get to know every student personally
- Open a private channel of communication with each learner
- Help students develop friendly relationships with each other
- Involve parents in three-way communication with you and their kids
- Prepare kids for state, PARCC, and Smarter Balanced tests
- Help kids connect with and learn from students around the world
- Inspire students to advocate and take action beyond the classroom
- Restore the enchantment, the flow, and the delight of teaching in hard times

Other than those things, letters aren't much use!

So, are you having a little "been-there-tried-that" moment right now? Probably everyone who's taught for more than a week has tried some kind of letters with his or her kids. Elementary teachers often try writing personal notes back and forth with students. Middle and high school teachers often have kids write literature letters" about their independent reading. And content-area teachers sometimes have kids write short notes in the form of admit slips or exit slips, handed in at the start or end of a class session.

But for most of us, these practices and other kinds of classroom correspondence somehow slipped away. Maybe we got overwhelmed by the sheer volume of letters the kids started sending us (in itself, a kind of proof of how much written conversations engage kids), or it simply slid out of our instructional routine under the crush of time, mandates, and new priorities.

So maybe we'll call this an old idea well worth reconsidering.

A NEW OLD IDEA

Of course, classroom note-writing, both licit and illicit, has a long history in our schools. Primary teachers have always treasured (and happily answered) endearing notes from their kids, like the one below.

As a first-grade teacher, what are you gonna write back? C-minus for the spelling? More like, "Elizabeth, I love how you drew the hearts going through your mind!"

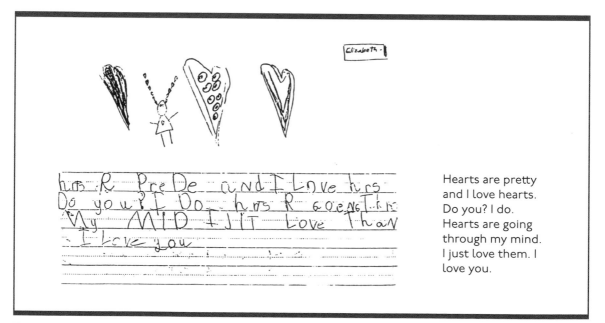

Hearts are pretty and I love hearts. Do you? I do. Hearts are going through my mind. I just love them. I love you.

Figure 1.1

Kids have also found ways to pass notes to each other in class (an 1890 discipline guide advises teachers to administer five lashes for this crime). Perhaps the classic of this genre is the "whatdja-get" note.

Figure 1.2

Maria's initial note to Omayra may be one of the archetypal letter types that kids have smuggled around classrooms since the beginning of time. But the girls' easy familiarity with standardized test questions is as fresh as today's headlines.

As kids get older, their notes to peers sometimes diverge even further from the curriculum. Here's one page of a longer middle school conversation.

Figure 1.3

The matchmaker seems to be having some difficulty in setting up Craig with a girl called Lovely. Craig, seriously, no interest?

The point is that our students are *already* engaged in almost constant letter-writing. They emit texts, instant messages, Facebook posts, and even the occasional dinosaur-era email. First graders at home are sending notes and pictures to their grandparents, and their pals across town. Teenagers are writing scores of texts, trying to plan for some excitement around our tiresome lessons.

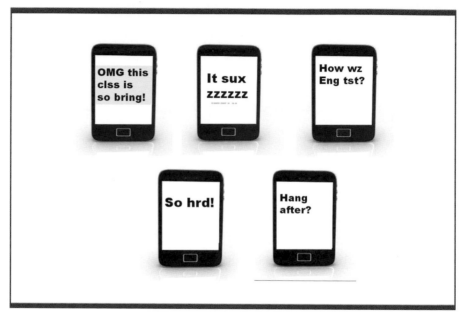

Figure I.4

Today's kids are writing letters ALL DAY LONG. They love it.

And, hey, if there is a form of communication that kids love, we teachers should exploit it immediately. If kids have a special vibration for that ancient/modern appeal of letters, a *frisson* for one-to-one writing, then let's get them corresponding—about the curriculum we are teaching.

Here's a kid-to-teacher note that is still personal and playful, but is also curriculum centered: It's a quick book review with some self-imposed alliteration practice for good measure.

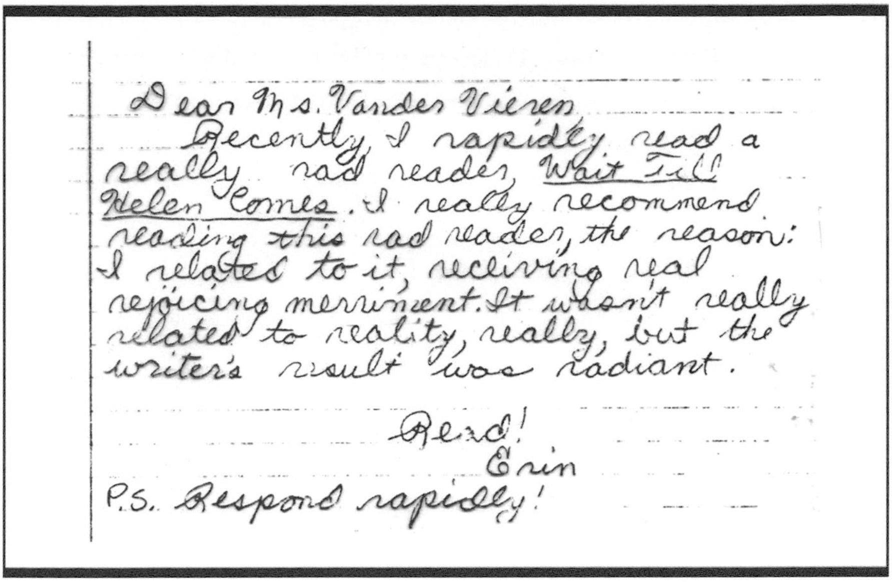

Dear Ms. Vander Vieren,
    Recently, I rapidly read a really rad reader, <u>Wait Till Helen Comes</u>. I really recommend reading this rad reader, the reason: I relate to it, receiving real rejoicing merriment. It wasn't really related to reality, really, but the writer's result was radiant.

        Read!
          Erin
P.S. Respond rapidly!

Figure I.5

We'll let 5-year-old author Andy Lopez conclude this demonstration.

Figure I.6

In this note especially written for his kindergarten teacher, Andy draws a cowboy (CBOY) and his wolf (WF)—or maybe it is a dog saying "woof"? We'd have to have a conference with Andy to sort that out. And then there is a big empty box labeled "write in here" (RTINHIR), which means *Please, teacher, write something in this special space I have made for you to answer my note!*

The takeaway: Kids are dying to get into written conversations with their teachers and their friends. Let's give them what they want!

NOTE to PRIMARY TEACHERS: Andy's note gives a clue to how we do written conversations in early childhood classrooms. We use drawing as the core and push in print as kids are capable. Stay tuned.

THOSE LETTERS ARE CUTE, BUT . . .

Most of the student samples we've shown so far are energetic, funny, and purposeful, but not exactly academic. So how do we put letter-writing to work in helping kids learn the curriculum? Please read the exchange in Figure 1.7 between third grader Kerri and her teacher Chris Smith.

Lucky Kerri, lucky Chris! Here is a teacher meeting a child's needs at so many levels that it almost makes your head spin. What a rich set of "mentor texts" Chris has created for this third grader, bathing her in the language of perfume, pearls, and sparkly things. She's modeling adult thinking, writing, spelling, penmanship, and conversation—targeted directly at Kerri's reading level and personal interests. In Common Core talk, we would call this a great lesson in explanatory writing.

While the official (and highly valuable) purpose of these daily "literature letters" is to support kids' independent reading, there's so much more going on. How deeply these two human beings are coming to know each other in this exchange.

Dear Mrs. Smith
    I like to play in
my moms clouse,
But   she says I
make   a   nes. I like
to   read   chapter Books
I   got   an   award
in   Where Does the sky
ends.

♡ Kerri

Dear Mrs. Smith

I like to play in my Mom's clothes, but she says I make a mess. I like to read chapter books. I got an award on *Where Does the Sky End*.

Love, Kerri

Dear Kerri,
    I saved some old formals
for my daughter Jen. She used to
love lipstick, powder, perfume &
curls- Also, she loved sparkly
things. (she still does) You are
a good reader. I'm happy you
read chap. books. Did you ever
read "Little House on the Prairie".
There's a whole series. I think
you might like.

♡ Mrs. Smith
nope I'v never read
LHOTP I think I could
try it out. I got
a new lunch box.
I like glow in the
dark stuff the most.
I think my sister is a
pain and every one
takes my money.
dose Jen ask for you
money. turn the
page

Mrs. Smith

Nope, I've never read LHOTP. I think I could try it out. I got a new lunch box. I like glow in the dark stuff the most. I think my sister is a pain and everyone takes my money. Does Jen ask for your money? Turn the page.

Figure I.7 (continued)

Figure 1.7 (continued)

I'm reading nocey druw books you so should try her she is a little piccy.

I'm reading Nancy Drew books now. You should try her. She is a little picky.

Dear Kerri,
Jenna loves to take my money! (she asks first ... she likes to buy clothes)
I LOVED Nancy Drew. I was older than you when I read them. I read all of them I think - but now I know they have more. She is picky. What's her boyfriends name - Ned?
♡ Mrs. Smith

Dear mrs smith In one of my Nancy Dr said she broke up and at the end she kissed Joe. I wish I'd look like Nancy.
♡ Kerri

Dear Mrs. Smith in one of my Nancy Drews it said she broke up and at the end she kissed Joe. I wish I'd look like Nancy. Love, Kerri

Dear Kerri,
When I was young, I always was jealous of Nancy because she seemed smart & always had a boyfriend & an exciting life! I think you are very pretty & I expect you will be a beautiful woman someday.
♡ Mrs. Smith

Figure 1.7

Our mentor-at-large Don Graves once said, "You are not ready to really teach a kid until you know 10 things about his or her life outside of school." How speedily Chris is reaching that threshold.

Yes, we did say *daily*. Chris chose to exchange notes almost every day with every student, meaning that by the end of the year every child in her class had received more than 150 letters from their teacher. Whew! Now, we can hear you wondering, "How many students did she have anyway? Less than me, I bet! How much time did she spend on this? Where am I supposed to find the time to do this with my kids?"

Your instincts are right—writing individual notes to your kids is undoubtedly powerful, but it can become an overwhelming task. Chris used kids' independent reading time each day to answer their letters; while they read books of choice, she wrote them notes. But that kind of frequency isn't required; a little goes a long way. We've found that writing personal notes to your class once a week is about all we, and most merely human teachers, can handle.

"Writing notes to just five kids a day allows for some very effective individual coaching, mentoring, and guiding."

But even in departmentalized middle and high schools, writing notes to just five kids a day still means that each student will get seven or eight personal letters from their teacher in a year. This is a fantastic step ahead of what we do now, and allows for some very effective individual coaching, mentoring, and guiding.

Far more important, over a school year and across the curriculum, is getting kids writing not to you, but to *each other*. Students must become each other's best audiences, correspondents, sounding boards, and debate partners. Written conversation only achieves its full value when your kids regularly and fluently write to each other in pairs, in small groups, on chart paper around a text, on bulletin boards, on the class blog, and more.

FAMILY HISTORY

We were both very fortunate young teachers, Smokey at Westinghouse in Chicago and Elaine at Lake Forest High School. Very early in our careers, we both discovered the power of written conversations.

Elaine: For many years I've had a big beautiful mailbox, decorated by an elementary school art club in Santa Fe. While I've always done letter-writing with my students, it's been a treat to have my own personal, portable mailbox. I've carried it to my various teaching stations all over New Mexico. In the classroom, I keep the mailbox, stationery and envelopes, markers, and sparkly crayons together so that students can write whenever they have a few extra minutes. These letters might be addressed to me or other students in the class, and stuffed into the mailbox. Someone stands the red flag up, and mail is delivered midday and again at the end of the day. Remember how magical it feels when you get a real live letter? That's what I want my students to enjoy every day.

Smokey: When I was a baby teacher, some consultant showed up at our school and suggested that we invite students into written conversations. His aim was mostly about providing socioemotional support, and he was sure right about kids deeply wanting to open up: In my first batch of kid letters, a boy confessed to heroin use (which I had to act on and which had a successful outcome). But I also noticed how engaged kids were when I had them write to each other about the social studies and literature topics we were studying in class. Since then, I have been using written conversations to replace those usually unengaging lectures and whole-class discussions. I have boxes of kids' amazing, brilliant, and hysterical letters from all over the United States saved in the family storage locker in Santa Fe.

KID-TO-KID LETTERS ABOUT THE CURRICULUM

Now, let's take a look at some kids having a written conversation with each other, not the teacher. Sara Ahmed's eighth-grade class in Chicago has been studying the origins of the Cold War and addressing the question, Which country was most responsible for initiating that conflict, the United States or the Soviet Union?

Today, Sara assigns students to read two short articles written in 1949, one by a Russian official named Dmitri Novikov and one by Henry Wallace, an American vice presidential candidate. Though these men drew different lessons from events, both acknowledged that America's use of nuclear weapons in Japan had horrified many countries around the world. As a result, some nations felt their only choice was to organize a mutual defense against the seemingly reckless and trigger-happy Americans. This idea—that the United States might once have been viewed as a bully by much of the world—was truly novel to Sara's 13-year-old students.

After kids read these eye-opening pieces, Sara asked them to join in an online written conversation for homework. "Everybody just get on our Edmodo site tonight and post once," she instructed, as kids filled their backpacks for the trip home.

Here are a few of the **83 posts** that resulted that night:

> **Sonali C.**—I think Henry Wallace was trying to turn America into a communist country. ☺ But, in all serious terms, I think Wallace was obviously on Novikov's side and I think it was wrong too, as he wasn't being patriotic to his own country (not saying everyone is. I'm not.) Maybe its because I'm an American, but I honestly think that America has its best intentions trying to make the world more peaceful. I think they do want more countries to be democratic but they don't want take over the world like the Soviet Union.
>
> Oct 6 | Edit | Delete

> **Max S.**—i disagree. I actually think that he wasn't. Throughout his speech, he had the same idea as Novikov, he thought that America just wanted power, which is want totalitarians want.
>
> Oct 6 | Edit | Delete

> **Teagan L.**—it was summarized, Max! His actual speech is probably a lot longer!
>
> Oct 6 | Edit | Delete

Isabel L.—i think i agree with Max. If you look at what Henry Wallace says, would you trust the U.S? Both sides wanted to spread their kind of government. Imagine what both situations were. If you are the Soviet Union, you want power, and "the fruits of war" but your opponent has atomic bombs! And if you are the U.S, you just really want to maintain countries democracies and build and rebuild new ones. I agree with all of you that i think it was both their faults, but whose do you think it was, PRIMARILY?

Oct 6 | Edit | Delete

Emmy S.—I think that there's a difference between being unpatriotic and disagreeing with some things that are happening in government. I don't think that Henry Wallace was purposely being unpatriotic; he was speaking out about what he thinks is wrong with the way the U.S. was acting during this time. If he was the Vice President, he wouldn't want America to completely change what it believes. I think he deserves more credit. It's really hard to stand up for what you believe in, or to give your opinion when you think someone or something is wrong. I see his speech as more of a, I don't know, wake up call, telling about how the U.S. might be portrayed to other countries.

I don't think he would completely turn on his own country and it's beliefs.

Oct 6 | Edit | Delete

Alejandro S.—But still c'mon, a lot of you people really need to re-read the Wallace speech. He isn't on the communist side, he doesn't want to spread communism, and he isn't on the Soviet Unions side either. Wallace is basically saying that we all look terrible in the eyes of the world. The U.S. used the atomic bomb to basically trash all of Nagasaki and Hiroshima, they entered World War 2 at the very last minute! The US was basically the game changer in war. He's saying that we are doing all these bad things and intimidating the rest of the world so they don't mess with us or are at least on our side. Why did they give Latin America weapons? It wasn't to be nice, it was basically a bribe to be on the United States side because Latin America needed weapons. The US is like, here we'll give you some weapons just to be "nice" Latin America would then return the favor by being on the U.S. side. If you all refer to your maps you'll see that all of Central American and South America is on the U.S side. Wallaces speech is a wake up call to the U.S to tell us all how we are portrayed by other countries which probably is the bully scaring other countries and trying to force Democracy on them like the Soviet Union is trying to force Communism on other countries

Oct 6 | Edit | Delete

Here we see students thinking together in just the way that our Common Core standards call for: They are taking positions, arguing them in writing, and using evidence from the texts in support of their positions. But this is no inert five-paragraph essay; the energy in this debate is palpable. These kids are not dutifully fulfilling a teacher command; they are driven by curiosity, and they are quite enthusiastically doing the kind of work historians actually do.

> *"Here we see students thinking together in just the way that our Common Core standards call for: taking positions, arguing, and using textual evidence."*

Later in the school year, Sara and her kids reflected back on both their out-loud small-group discussions and their written conversations, and they co-created this chart. Look at the attributes they noticed in each variety of discussion.

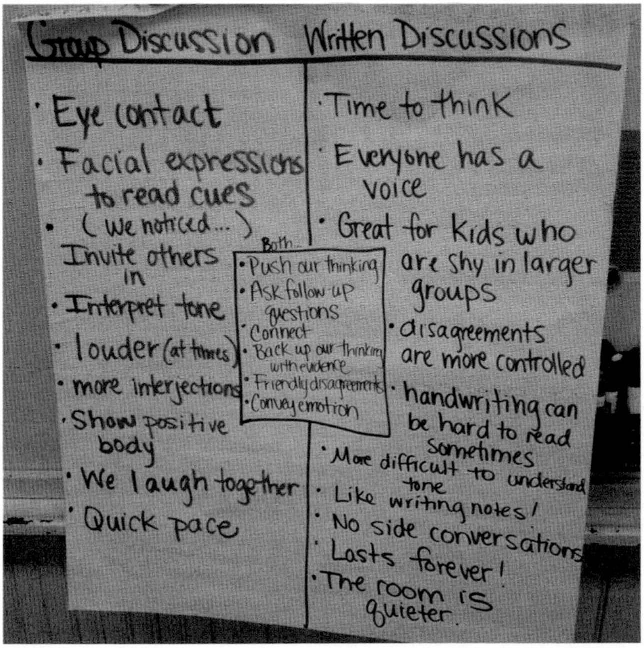

Figure 1.8

This chart speaks volumes. First, it shows that Sara's kids see spoken and written discussion as two sides of the same coin: both necessary and valuable and both with different advantages. But the right-hand column reveals some profound and unrecognized benefits of discussions that happen in writing.

- You can think before you "speak."

- No one can be silenced. No "hog" can suck up all the air; everybody gets the same amount of time with his or her blank sheet of paper. Nobody can interrupt you.

- Kids who are reluctant to speak aloud have a way into the conversation.

- There's less danger of yelling or bullying.

- It's like writing notes = it's fun!

- No distracting side conversations are possible (think how often "live" classroom discussions get undermined by such chitchat!).

- There is quiet that enhances concentration. When you read and respond to others' notes, you can focus on their words and their thinking.

- Unlike conversations that evaporate into the air, written conversations leave a permanent record of the thinking.

Amid all the benefits, the kids also acknowledge some challenges with handwriting and understanding people's tone in writing, versus out-loud speaking.

Now look what's in the center: all the things that *both* kinds of discussions can provide.

Push our thinking

Ask follow-up questions

Connect

Back up our thinking with evidence

Friendly disagreements

Convey emotion

We have our own version of the kids' chart. It isn't any smarter, but it is longer (see pages 18 and 19).

MEETING THE COMMON CORE STATE STANDARDS WITH LETTERS

How can written conversations help our kids to meet the Common Core State Standards or the quite similar goals in non-Core states like Texas, Virginia, and Minnesota? Actually, the four writing models described in this book are not just helpful, but *vital* in helping students reach college and career readiness not just in writing, but in reading, speaking, and listening as well. While the K–12 literacy standards are highly integrated, we will try to pull them apart a bit here just to show how written conversations move kids ahead.

Writing Standards

The Common Core wants writing to be fully equal with reading in the time and attention it receives in school. That means that teachers must provide far more writing practice, experience, and instruction than students have typically gotten. Periodically crafting extended, formal, edited pieces is clearly required. But the Core also wants students to get constant practice with shorter forms of writing.

> *"The Common Core wants writing to be fully equal with reading in the time and attention it receives in school."*

Writing Anchor Standard 10 (2012) asks that students "Write routinely over extended time frames (time for research, reflection, and revision) and shorter time frames (a single sitting or a day or two) for a range of tasks, purposes, and audiences." But most of the other writing standards focus on students composing scattered formal pieces to be painstakingly assessed and edited by teachers. But to become fluent, confident, proficient writers, students need far more writing practice than teachers can ever grade. Kids should be writing not every few weeks, but three, six, ten times *a day*. We think the Common Core really missed the boat on this subject, setting a way-too-low standard for writing practice.

WHY LETTERS ARE SUCH A POWERFUL TEACHING TOOL

Letters are *fun*. They invite you to express your personality directly—to put your unique thinking on the page or the screen. Indeed, letters are sometimes more revealing than the author intends or realizes.

Letters are all about the *audience*. When we write a note or email, we visualize the intended receiver's face, think about their reaction, and, above all, anticipate their response.

Letters are *purposeful*. They are almost always about getting some work done in the world—to arouse ardor, plan a trip, solve a problem, air some issues.

Letters are *private*. Most letters are intended for just one other person; it's strictly *entre nous*; there are taboos against opening others' mail. Secrets are a big part of letter history.

Letters are always an *artwork*, as well as a piece of communication: Every letter is a small work of art, handmade. We sometimes fuss over stationery, envelopes, the feel and shape of the paper. Precious letters may be saved for a lifetime. And now, with emails and texts, we can still decorate with fonts, emoticons, and photos.

Letters have enjoyable *rituals and conventions*, some of which are archaic in a good way: special paper, ink, letter forms, salutations, closings, seals, upside-down stamps—and their digital equivalents.

Letters invite *reflection*. One convention of letters is that they combine reporting on life events with analyzing, interpreting, and making sense of them. Note how often people make declarations, confessions, or important statements in a letter.

In an exchange of letters, *airtime is equal*. No one can dominate the discussion as they do in an out-loud conversation. Both correspondents can take as much space and time as they need to say what they want.

While you are writing a letter, the person you are addressing *cannot interrupt you*.

Letters create their own *space and time*, a temporary world that writers and readers co-create; you have to break the spell at the end (e.g., "Well, I have to go back to my math homework now . . .").

When writing a letter, you can be *more thoughtful,* taking time, care, deliberation, and planning to what you say. This is why we often discover what we really think (or dare to say momentous things) in a letter.

You can't unsay words that fall out of your mouth, but you can revise a letter before mailing it or pressing send. You can *revise*, edit, and get it just right, just the way you want it, before launching it off to the reader. Similarly, the recipient can reread, study, and reflect upon your letter before responding.

Letters are *eternal*. Culture pundits are always declaring letter-writing to be "a lost art" that is dying out in today's corrupt culture, blah blah blah. But *letters always come back from the dead*. Witness the recent booms of email, and then texting, and then Twitter, and next, who knows?

Letters *change the world,* and will continue to do so. For just one example, Martin Luther King's "Letter From Birmingham Jail," addressed to his fellow clergymen (and all of America), was a turning point in the civil rights movement—and now that letter is studied by almost every student in our country.

When students regularly join in structured written conversations with their teachers and peers, they get vital practice in thoughtful expression, the language of discussion and response, the process of building knowledge and analyzing ideas, ways of seeking evidence and developing supports, and presenting their thinking to a real, responsive audience. They are also under significant pressure to follow language, spelling, and organizational conventions, to be sure that their ideas can be easily understood by the various audiences who will be reading them.

The Common Core has especially high aims for the neglected modes of argumentative and explanatory writing. There's a huge premium placed upon students' ability to dig deep into a complex text and take a position, to develop an argument based upon evidence inside it, and to go public with well-reasoned and smoothly written arguments.

Look back to pages 13–15 and review the conversation among those middle school kids about the Cold War. They are staking out and defending positions, and supporting them with evidence from their two readings, trying to draw justifiable inferences from sources. Notice how the kids sometimes boldly question each other's evidence or scold other people's reasoning. Alejandro really holds his classmates' feet to the fire: "But still c'mon, a lot of you people really need to re-read the Wallace speech." And later he advises: "If you all refer to your maps you'll see that all of Central American and South America is on the U.S side . . ." Written conversations like these are a made-to-order tool for developing first drafts of argument and explanation papers.

More broadly, students who have frequent opportunities to engage in extended written conversations are developing the fluency, confidence, stamina, and audience awareness they need to grow as writers. And they are also receiving the kind of immediate feedback that developing writers need, not just for initial motivation, but to grow and improve steadily. This is writing that's real, writing that has consequences—and writing that's engaging.

Reading Standards

The Common Core states that students at all grade levels should be reading more nonfiction text and more complex texts in all genres and should enjoy less teacher "spoon-feeding." Kids should be challenged to make meaning from within the four corners of the text, without teachers cuing them in advance what to look for.

We also know from decades of research that students understand text better—and get better scores on individual standardized tests—when they have a chance to talk about their reading with classmates (Allington, 2012). Indeed, this is one strategy that proficient adult readers typically use when they are grappling with some challenging text; they seek others with whom to discuss it, they talk to someone, they "phone a friend."

Getting in the habit of verbalizing your thinking as you read transfers to your cognitive repertoire; the more aware kids become of their own thinking (their connections, their inferences, their visualizations), the better readers they become, with others and on their own.

Jack Hollingsworth/Thinkstock.

Speaking and Listening Standards

In our near panic to address the reading and writing standards, many teachers have overlooked the potentially transformational Common Core State Standards for Speaking and Listening. Among the goals for students at all ages are performances like the following:

> Engage effectively in a range of collaborative discussions (one-on-one, in groups, and teacher-led) with diverse partners on grade level topics and texts, building on others' ideas and expressing their own clearly.

> Come to discussions prepared, having read or studied required material; explicitly draw on that preparation and other information known about the topic to explore ideas under discussion. (National Governors Association Center for Best Practices and the Council of Chief State School Officers, 2010, pp. 24, 49)

In other words, having our students discuss curricular ideas in small groups isn't an option under the Common Core; it is a straight-up *mandate*. You must do it and make it work. And one of the most effective structures we have for facilitating that kind of peer discussion is—guess what?—written conversations.

And let's remember some other things those eighth graders taught us with their chart: Written discussions equalize airtime, invite in the shy kids, prohibit side conversations, allow you to be more thoughtful, and "last forever," leaving tangible, assessable evidence of each child's thinking.

ENGAGEMENT, BEST PRACTICE, AND WRITTEN CONVERSATIONS

Now, let's think beyond the Common Core to the more general and eternal question: What does best practice teaching really look like? How can we set up classrooms and provide instruction so that kids learn deeply? Smokey and his colleagues Steve Zemelman and Arthur Hyde, in reviewing all the research on educational "best practice," have identified the main attributes: classrooms where learners are genuinely engaged with experiences that are challenging, authentic, collaborative, and conceptual (Zemelman, Daniels, and Hyde, 2012).

But despite decades of research, a good deal of school time is still allocated to lessons in which the teacher either lectures to a silent class or holds "whole-class discussions," during which a handful of students volunteer answers while the majority sleep. When the teacher is the "sage on the stage," there is little positive social pressure for kids to commit, to participate, to join in the thinking. But no matter how ineffective, being that sage is still really hard work for us as teachers.

But have you ever heard that supposedly comedic phrase "School is a place where young people go to watch old people work?" While this notion grates on our every teacherly nerve, it does have some truth. Too often in school, we teachers *are* doing all the work—performing, presenting, spoon-feeding, cajoling, entertaining, *all day long*—while kids sit and watch, free to daydream and catch up on sleep.

Teachers who begin using written conversations during class are often amazed at how hard their kids are suddenly working. Engagement is built in; it comes standard. The structure is inherently involving: You get to write to a friend or two about a topic that's interesting. When you sit down with a partner or a small group, there's a high degree of positive social pressure to participate. You've got a classmate beside you who's expecting a letter from you in just a minute—and a kid on your other side who's about to send one to you. Being in a live letter exchange is brisk, fast-paced, and demanding of focus and attention. You're in the middle of an active process that depends on your cooperation.

Teachers are also a bit surprised that during written conversations, they are actually free to wander the room, observe students at work, look over shoulders, and think about the activity. When you stop entertaining and get "off stage," for more than a second or two, it's a whole different world. As one delighted teacher told us, "The kids get so into these written conversations, I could probably go check my email if I wanted." That would be wrong, but it's often true: Written conversations are among the most challenging and kid-engaging structures we can mount in our classrooms.

In short, there is an imbalance in schools. We have lots of out-loud talk by teachers with low accountability for kids. Instead, we need much more written discussion by students with high levels of social and academic pressure to join in, think hard, and leave evidence of their thinking.

HOW THE BOOK IS ORGANIZED

In this introductory section, we have been trumpeting the benefits of curricular letter-writing, offering student samples, reviewing roots and research, and promising you many happy endings if you start using this interactive tool. In the book, we will show you four versions of written conversations, moving basically from early-in-the-year versions to later ones, from simpler to more complex (we prefer *elegant*), and from inside-the-classroom letters to correspondence that reaches out to the world.

Coming up next is a crucial and unrecognized application of written conversations: creating personal, friendly, supportive, and responsible relationships among your students at the start of the year (and all year long).

Chapter 2. A Community of Correspondents. Letters are a vital tool for building collaborative relationships in the classroom. We use correspondence to build acquaintance and friendship, to negotiate expectations and share responsibilities. To this end, we deploy letters between teachers and kids, kids and kids, and kids and teachers and parents; we share news journals; we set up classroom mail systems and message boards; and we write teacher-to-whole-class messages.

Next come four chapters that each addresses a specific type of written conversation that has proved useful in K–12 classrooms: mini memos, dialogue journals, write-arounds, and digital discussions.

Each of these chapters follows a similar template, offering the following:

- A **definition** of the structure
- An explanation of its **origins and research base**
- A **"quick look"** at a classic student sample
- A full **launching lesson** that shows the writing at work inside a real curricular topic, with teaching language you can try for yourself
- A generic, **step-by-step instruction** sheet for any teaching situation
- Detailed information on several **subtypes and variations**
- A list of practical **management and problem-solving tips**
- Plenty of **student samples** of this kind of letter in kids' (and teachers') own words

Chapter 3. Mini Memos. This is our name for the familiar family of admit slips, start-up writes, exit slips, and midclass writing breaks. These classic writing-to-learn jottings have always been implicitly letters; an exit slip is essentially a note to the teacher telling "what I learned today" or "what questions I have." We leverage up the value of these quick notes when we give them official audiences and responders.

Chapter 4. Dialogue Journals. This is about pairs or partners—just two people—corresponding. We start small before we invite kids into write-arounds in larger groups. Dialogue journals can be either kid-teacher or kid-kid. Curricular conversations with peers are the primary use, but we can also engage students in correspondence with us, in which we coach, give feedback, or even address behavior issues.

Chapter 5. Write-Arounds. Also called written conversation or silent literature circles. Here, groups of three or four (rarely more) join in discussions of academic content—books, concepts, lab experiments—any common experience. These conversations happen in individual letters passed around a table, or on big sheets of chart paper where kids converse in the margins. Usually, these conversations switch from silent to aloud after a period of sustained silent writing.

Chapter 6. Digital Discussions. This chapter covers the tech-enabled versions of many forms in Chapters 3 through 5, plus correspondence that is uniquely digital, like email, texts, blog posts, and more.

LET THE STUDENT SAMPLES TEACH YOU

Over the past few months, we often joked that we were writing a *picture book,* not a professional text. And that's partly true. Inspired by Lucy Calkins' beautiful and groundbreaking *The Art of Teaching Writing* (1986), we've stuffed the book with scores of kid conversations, mostly in their own writing and drawing. A piece of student writing is always an artifact and often an artwork. Whatever it communicates, a letter exists as a made thing, perfect for a refrigerator door or a gallery wall. The samples we've chosen fully reveal the power and practicality of written conversation. If you let them, the kids' writings will guide you just as effectively as the lessons, instructions, and tips we have also compiled here.

In a few spots, we have provided translations of kids' handwriting; this helps those of us who do not speak the foreign language called "invented spelling" to appreciate primary children's written conversations. We've also inserted marginal comments where we could illuminate students' thinking, their writing strategies, and their social interactions.

So please slow down and enjoy the kids' writing on its own terms: Savor the energy, notice the purposefulness, laugh at the intentional and the inadvertent jokes, notice the gentle gestures of friendship, applaud when the thinking deepens, and cringle at the spelling—but keep your red pen in its holster for just a while. Enjoy!

Sincerely yours,
Smokey and Elaine

P.S. Please be in touch with us via www.harveydaniels.com.

Dear Reader,

In the beginning of the school year, we use those precious early days and weeks to create our "classroom climate"— the atmosphere of friendliness, support, mutual respect, and collaboration that makes everything possible in the months to come. We already know that adolescents will text each other all day long, while primary kids address love notes to their teachers. Let's put that letter-loving urge to work in the service of community!

Smokey and Elaine

WE'VE GOT MAIL

We try to live up to Donald Graves's challenge that until you know 10 things about each kid on your roster, you are not ready to teach them. But man, that's a tall order when you have 30 kids in your class—and *especially* if you are a secondary teacher with 150 faces passing through your room daily! But Graves was right; the more you know kids, the better you can teach them.

But how can you get all that information? And collect it promptly, at the start of a school year, so you can put it to work? And remember it? One answer, of course, is letters—what a great, natural venue for sharing and exchanging personal information. Of course, when building our classroom community, there are many steps we can take that are face-to-face and out-loud. But there are some special and powerful ways in which letters, and the written conversations within them, can work significant magic.

VARIATIONS:
- Back-to-School Letters
- Parent and Kid Letters
- Message Boards
- Class Stationery
- Shields
- Topic Journals
- Classroom and School Mail Systems
- Teacher-Student Friendly Letters
- Student-Student Friendly Letters
- Multi-Age Friendly Letters

Here's why this is so important. Any new classful of kids typically arrives *asymmetrically prepared to collaborate*. Some students know and like each other, others know and dislike each other, and still others don't know each other at all, but hold suspicions, reservations, or stereotypes about each other. If we want a class where everyone works seamlessly with everyone else all year long, we cannot let this situation stand. We must actively put kids together so they can become better acquainted, overcome mutual ignorance, and leave old beefs behind.

Sounds like an uphill struggle, right? But here's what we have working for us: Social psychology (and life) teaches us that *we like people we know*. By and large, the more we get to know other people, the more we like them—and vice versa. This is one of the most adorable traits of our species. Acquaintance generally leads to friendliness, and friendliness leads to supportive behavior. So if we are teachers seeking a collaborative classroom climate, then we are in the friendship-building business whether we like it or not. And we do like it!

We want everyone, kids and teachers and even parents, having friendly written conversations with each other at the start of the school year, or whenever we are working toward more cohesive classrooms.

Right now you might be asking, "What if I'm in the middle of the year and my kids don't get along well enough to work together? Can I still use letters to build or improve my classroom community?" Absolutely. You don't need to wait until next fall. While first encounters undeniably do provide a fertile time to build relationships, we can work on friendliness and support any time of the year. Indeed, many teachers do start working on collaboration issues at mid-year, when they become worried about the morale or climate of the classroom. It's always a good time to advance that acquaintance-friendliness-support cycle among our students.

BACK-TO-SCHOOL LETTERS

Before we even lay eyes on our kids, we can begin corresponding and getting to know them. Many smart teachers we know send welcome letters to each of their students' homes a couple of weeks before the first day of school. Typically, these letters, which come as a happy surprise in August, include several ingredients. The teacher tells a little bit about him- or herself, previews some of the cool things the class will be learning about (plants, Shakespeare, etc.), and then invites kids (and, for the younger ones, parents) to respond.

Around the middle of August, Michele Timble drops 30-odd notes into her neighborhood mailbox. On one side of the page is her greeting and invitation; on the other are ready-made boxes for families to fill out.

Dear Room 303 Parents,

Debbie Miller, a nationally known teacher, researcher, and author I respect, has eloquently described my intentions for your kids' first month of school.

> "For me, September is all about building relationships, establishing trust, creating working literate environments, and getting to know children as readers and learners."

As I work to get to know your children, I invite you to write to me about them. I ask that you share anything you think it is important for me to know (school related or not!). Knowing your child's talents, likes, dislikes, and more helps me be a better teacher for them and increases the likelihood that they'll experience success.

So please take a few minutes (on the back of this paper) to tell me what I might not know by watching them walk through our doors next week. Children are invited to co-author with you if they like!

I look forward to our year together. Thank you.

Mrs. T

Within days, responses start piling up from enthusiastic parents and kids (see Figures 2.1 and 2.2).

Of course, Michele could also do this by email—and she does often use that tool in corresponding with kids and families. But at the start of the acquaintance, the hand-made physical letters have a living, down-home quality that's hard to create digitally.

Bigger kids also enjoy—and are even more surprised—when a teacher sends them a before-school letter. Like, is this for real?

Three things you should know about
_____Dominic_____(student's name)

1. Dominic is _very_ interested in sports and history (e.g., the Titanic, Chicago, etc) and is far more motivated in school when studying Things that interest him!

2. Dominic is a smart kid, but has a hard time staying focused in school especially in areas where he struggles (e.g. reading + writing). As a result he rushes through to get done vs. taking time to do it right. We'd like to see him slow down, Think things Through _first_ and ask for help when he needs it (e.g., if a word or question confuses him) so That he can do it right/well The first time vs. being frustrated by rework/bad grades.

3. Dominic has a sense of humor + likes to laugh and make others laugh.

Completed by _Katie Spilotro (mom)_

4. (bonus) Dominic likes to be a part of The conversation. We've trying to help him find kind and inclusive ways to communicate so That he makes others feel good vs. feeling That he's "had The last word."

Look how much valuable and specific information Mom Katie has to offer. She's making it way easier for Michele to reach and teach Dominic. A teacher could take weeks trying to infer all this information from a student's behavior—back-to-school letters allow a huge jump start. They also offer a "heart connection" between teacher and parent that almost always proves valuable later on.

Figure 2.1

> **Three things you should know about**
> __Priscilla__ (student's name)
>
> 1. I love sports!
>   Priscilla is a very kind, gentle and compassionate person. She loves to learn and is diligent. She especially loves to learn music.
>
> 2. My Family is very big
>   She learns best in quiet setting, hands on is good
>
> 3. I love pasta!!!
>   She has two brothers, a dog and wants a zoo in our house. She has a huge heart especially for animals.
>
> **Completed by** __Priscilla__ & mom Chinue

Doubly valuable when kids co-author!   Figure 2.2

Dear Denizens of Room 115,

I am Mrs. Daniels, and I will be your freshman English teacher for this year. Don't remember me? That's because I wasn't on the faculty last year. I just moved to New Mexico, but I'm not new to the classroom. I spent the past 20 years teaching in Chicago, and I'll be glad to tell you all about the Windy City!

I'm looking forward to meeting all of you young scholars, and finding out what you are interested in. Meanwhile, here's a list of fascinating facts about me (well, I think they are).

1. I have a pet rabbit called Oreo.

2. I have a daughter who is 29 years old and is an artist.

3. My son is 35 and owns his own pathology company (you don't want to know).

4. My husband Harvey writes books for teachers.

5. When I was a child, I played Bach on the organ.

6. My favorite country other than the USA is Italy.

7. I like to cook New Mexican food, and my pulled pork is the best. The very best. Like don't argue with me, totally the best.

8. I drive a 12-year-old Toyota with 116,000 miles on it.

9. My hobby is reading novels on my Kindle.

10. I listen to country music, and I ain't apologizin' for it!

What 10 things can you tell me about *you*?? Please write back or send me an email.

Finally, here's a little mental homework: When we get together next week, we will make a class constitution—some rules to live by to make this school year more fun and interesting. So be thinking about some suggestions you could offer when we have that conversation.

See you on the 16th!

Mrs. Elaine Daniels

Kids love it when teachers self-disclose, proving that they are (at least somewhat) human. But choose your disclosures wisely!

This is your chance to let kids know the kind of collaborative culture you hope to create.

If this is an email, you can easily pop in a picture of your dog or your home library—whatever applies to your kids and your grade level. Or write about the best books you read during the summer, or where you traveled, or what family projects you completed.

PARENT AND KID LETTERS

Did you notice how young Priscilla jumped into the back-to-school letter in Figure 2.2? She reminds us that parents make great letter-writing partners, too. Duh! Think how often we harangue parents to read, read, read with their kids! But we far less often suggest they write with them too, which is every bit as important.

Our two lucky kids went to Baker Demonstration School, where the teachers always encouraged intrafamily correspondence. Figure 2.3 is a note that Smokey and 8-year-old Marny passed back and forth over the car seat during a long road trip, as Elaine drove.

So one helpful thing we can do at the start of the year is get parents involved in written conversations with their kids—and us. Some teachers establish three-way parent-child-teacher journals early in the year that regularly travel from home to school. Usually the underlying topic is what I am doing/learning in school, inviting all parties to get into written conversation about highlights, successes, enthusiasms, challenges, and planning.

MESSAGE BOARDS

Once we get kids into the room with us, the correspondence can begin in earnest. Sure, we will get acquainted face-to-face, but we'll extend and deepen our connections through letters. At Columbine Elementary School in Boulder,

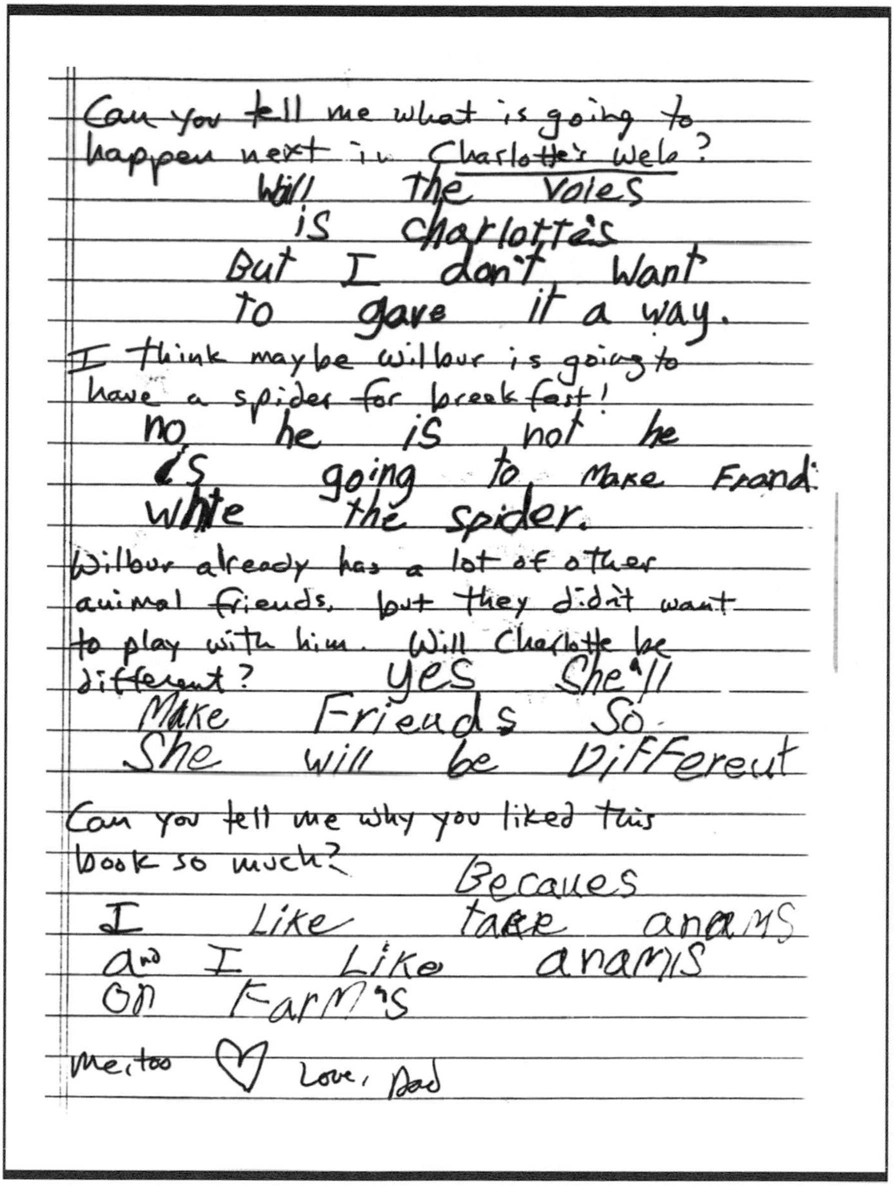

Can you tell me what is going to
happen next in Charlotte's web?
Will The Voles
is charlottes
But I don't want
To gave it a way.
I think maybe wilbur is going to
have a spider for breakfast!
no he is not he
is going to make Frand:
white the spider.
Wilbur already has a lot of other
animal friends. but they didn't want
to play with him. Will Charlotte be
different? yes She'll
Make Friends So
She will be Different

Can you tell me why you liked this
book so much? Becaues
I Like tarr anams
and I Like anamis
on Farms
me,too ♡ Love, Dad

Don't worry, we won't fill the *whole* book with our own children's precious writings. But this shows how simple and casual it can be for parents to have written book talks with their kids—and it encourages the parents to the read the books, too.

Figure 2.3

Colorado, second-grade teacher Brad Buhrow has a message board set up on the first day of school. He stands beside an empty rectangle of poster board and then writes a note in the center: "Write to Brad!" He explains that kids are invited to write him a note anytime. Notes can be any combination of words and drawings that gets the meaning across. They might be some news from home, a question that came up during class, or a request of the teacher ("Can I share my writing today?"). Brad promises that he will write an answer to every note the same day. All the tools—variously sized Post-its and skinny markers—are stored right nearby.

The kids can't wait to get into a written conversation with Brad and their classmates. They come up at the start of the day, during breaks, after lunch, during writing workshop, or just before bus time to post their thoughts. As the day progresses, Brad periodically stops by the board to read messages and quickly

Kids are invited to post notes to Brad on the message board and to attach anything else they'd like him to respond to, such as small artworks, photos, or cards.

Figure 2.4

respond to a few. He reserves one color of Post-its for himself (this week, it's orange), so kids can easily see his responses appearing on the board.

Brad supports students' use of the message board in many ways. Because some of his kids are English language learners and others aren't yet strong readers, Brad will visit the message board with those kids, helping them to read the messages and join the conversation with a picture or a few words. During class lessons, if a student comes up with a great question (or is distracting everyone from the job at hand), Brad might say, "What an interesting idea. Will you go write that on the message board so we can all think about it?"

Every couple of weeks, when the board is filled, Brad takes it down and puts up a fresh new space. Sometimes he'll create a colorful, inviting design; other times he'll give kids a broad, open-ended topic to jump-start a new conversation; and still other times, he just lets kids find their own way. "The message board is hugely popular in my room," he reports. "It's a great forum for connecting, thinking, making art, and publically sharing ideas. The kids enjoy it because it is completely voluntary—no scoring, no rubrics. Since I believe the foundation of literacy is choice, this is an important part of my classroom." Brad's main suggestion: "It won't work if you don't write back. You have to read and think about what the kids are saying. Then stay on it."

CLASSROOM STATIONERY

Our Chicago friends Michele Timble and Debbie King get their fourth graders excited about letter-writing by creating special classroom stationery.

All students in each class create a cartoon version of themselves, then Deb and Michele resize and paste everyone's likeness into a beautiful border for Room

What a beautiful and easy idea. Personalized stationery just for your class. You could add the room number, mailing address, or blog site too.

Figure 2.5

303 and Room 305 versions. They keep an ample supply of this personalized paper in their classroom writing centers. Grab a sheet and let the writing begin!

SHIELDS

Michele's got another letter-based activity for starting the year and building acquaintance. First, she takes a snapshot of each kid and prints it out from the classroom computer. Then, she sticks each picture on a blank "shield," and hangs these shields at well-spaced intervals throughout the room.

Now, kids bring a pen, and each one stands in front of another classmate's shield. They write one thing they appreciate about that person, in one of the shield sections. Then, when Michele says, "Go," they rotate to the next face in the gallery of classmates, and write something complimentary again. Four stops, four minutes. She encourages students to add specific details about what makes each person valuable, not just "She's nice." This way, everyone gets several positive comments—there are no "popular" kids who get 20 praises while others get zero.

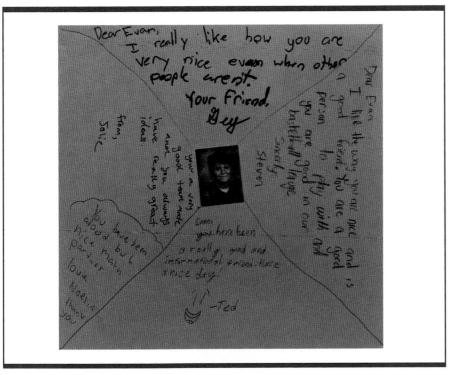

What do we learn about Evan? A good basketball player and teammate, a steadfast friend, very "informational," and a "good but loud" math partner. High praise!

Figure 2.6

Now we are generally wary of activites that ask kids to just "make nice" with each other. People grow from having their *accomplishments* validated, not having their mere existence praised. But here we appreciate how specific and sincere the kids are.

Here are a few comments from other shields:

You are such a great buddy and you're a great wordsmith/Batman buddy!

I Like that you are never a poor sport at recess.

You are a great inquiry circle partener. Thanks for helping me glue down my cards.

Thank you for all you've done for me. When I need a laugh I can always come to you. And when I'm down you can always cheer me up.

You have a great hairdo in that picture. Now let's get to businsss, you are a great friend and have a great personality. You rock! Go Thunder!

You have been such a good science parner recently in research workshop and you are always on topic!

You always let it go when I accidentally say something mean. Like when I am talking to someone and push you off.

You always when I am looking glum or sad ask "What's wrong" or "are you OK?" which always makes me feel good.

Of course, the teacher has a shield up as well . . .

You are a grate teacher, you help me learn math and recherch.

You teachd me a lot of crusive and you are the best!

Now, time for some spelling?

Building on this history of supportive correspondence, Michele and Debbie's kids can write to each other all year long.

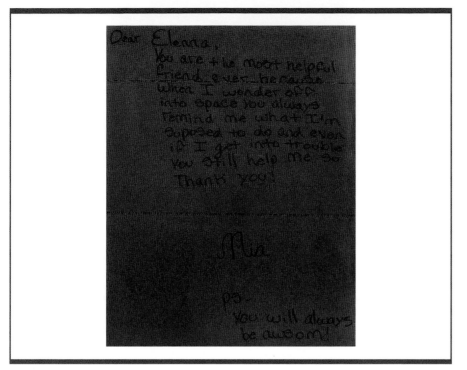

Dear Elena,
You are the most helpful
friend ever because
when I wonder off
into space you always
remind me what I'm
supposed to do and even
if I get into trouble
you still help me so
Thank you!

Mia

ps.
You will always
be awsom!

Figure 2.7

Dear, Guy October, 25, 201

Thank you for comforting
me when I thought I lost
my balaclava (hat thingy).

Sincerley,
Griffin

Dear Guy, Thank you for comforting me when I thought I lost my balaclava (hat thingy). Sincerely, Griffin

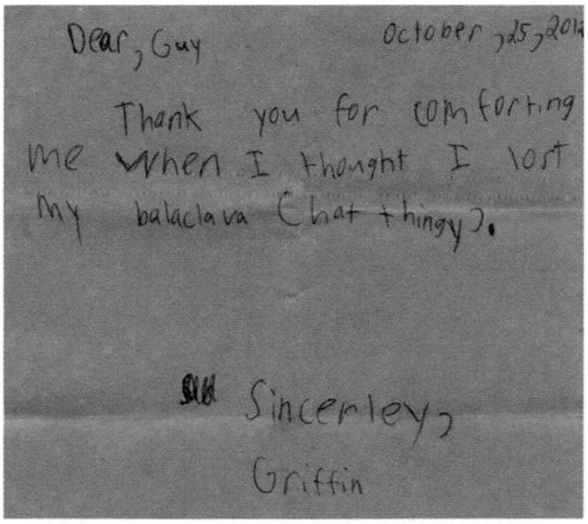

Figure 2.8

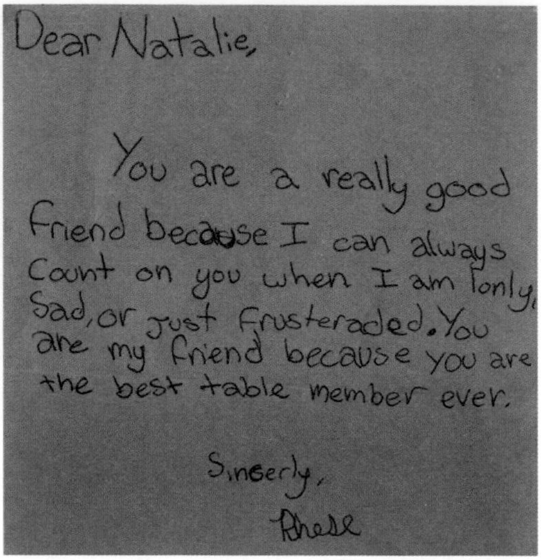

Dear Natalie,

You are a really good friend because I can always count on you when I am lonly, sad, or just frusteraded. You are my friend because you are the best table member ever.

Sincerly,

Rhese

Figure 2.9

TOPIC JOURNALS

OK, just one more Marny story. When our daughter was in third grade, she had a marvelous teacher named Theresa Kubasak, who really believed in kids writing to each other. One unique outlet she offered was a set of blank journals kept in the back of the classroom. Each one was labeled for writing about a special topic:

The Book of Pets

The Book of Sisters and Brothers

The Book of Funny Jokes

The Book of Injuries and Accidents

The Book of Grandparents

The Book of Family Trips

The Book of Death

What? That last journal topic sure caught our attention when we first walked into Theresa's classroom. But, as she cogently explained, many of the kids in her classes had experienced the deaths of pets, and some grandparents, and that *dying* was a big, urgent topic that some kids needed to write about.

During freewriting time, students could choose to go back to the journal area, find the book that suited their interests at that moment, and write an entry. Then, the next visitor to that journal (a student or Mrs. Kubasak) would read what the previous writer had said, and respond, react, or comment. In other words, by picking one of the journals a child could enter voluntary written conversations with others in the class on issues of common interest or concern. Though this is a gorgeously effective community-building tool, we've rarely seen teachers using topic journals since then—and our daughter is 28 now!

So we were especially delighted to meet Julie Hochman at Disney II Magnet School in Chicago last year. She's doing the same thing with second graders, and she shared some samples with us. Here's the cover of her classroom's family journal.

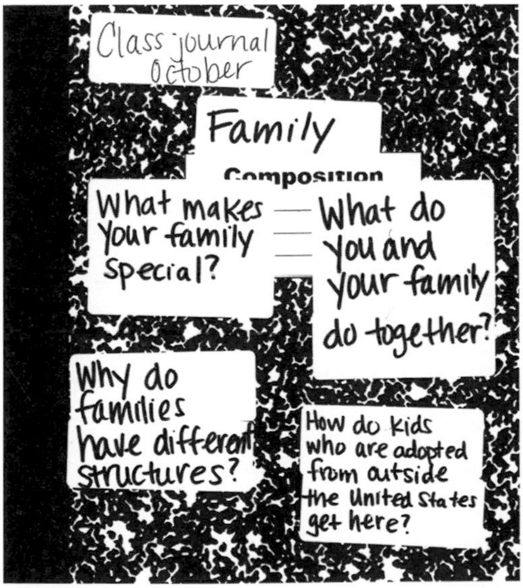

Notice how Julie has primed the pump with good family-related questions.

Figure 2.10

Connor shows us how easy it is to make a visit to the family journal.

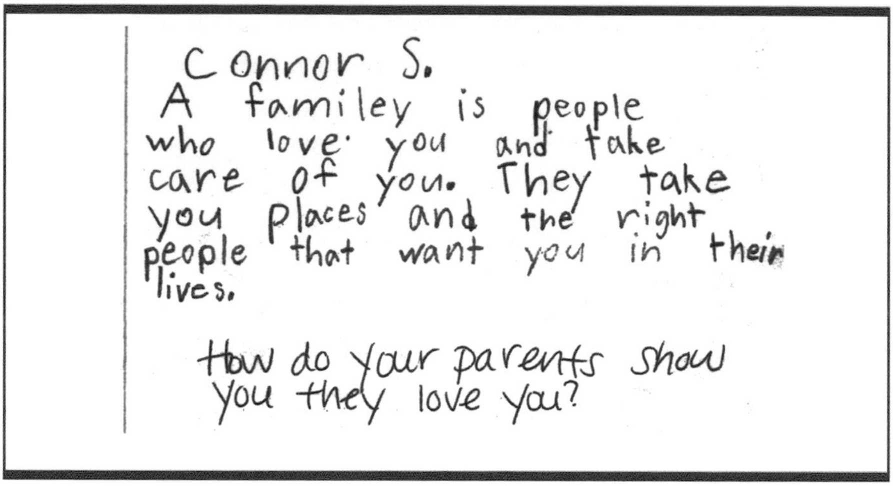

> Connor S.
> A familey is people who love you and take care of you. They take you places and the right people that want you in their lives.
>
> How do your parents show you they love you?

Figure 2.11

Julie often enters the discussion and supports kids' ongoing conversations (see Figure 2.12).

For these topic journals to succeed at any grade level, it is especially important for teachers to be "present" in the pages, modeling relevant responses, demonstrating adult writing, stirring up the conversation, and responding to individual kids' needs.

CLASSROOM AND SCHOOL MAIL SYSTEMS

Elaine: The first time I encountered a classroom mail system was about 20 years ago. I was in a third-grade class in Wilmette, Illinois, and I noticed homemade folders with the kids' names on them, glued to the side of their desks. They were made out of manila folders, decorated up and hung. I was observing a student teacher at the time, and before I left, I delightedly wrote her

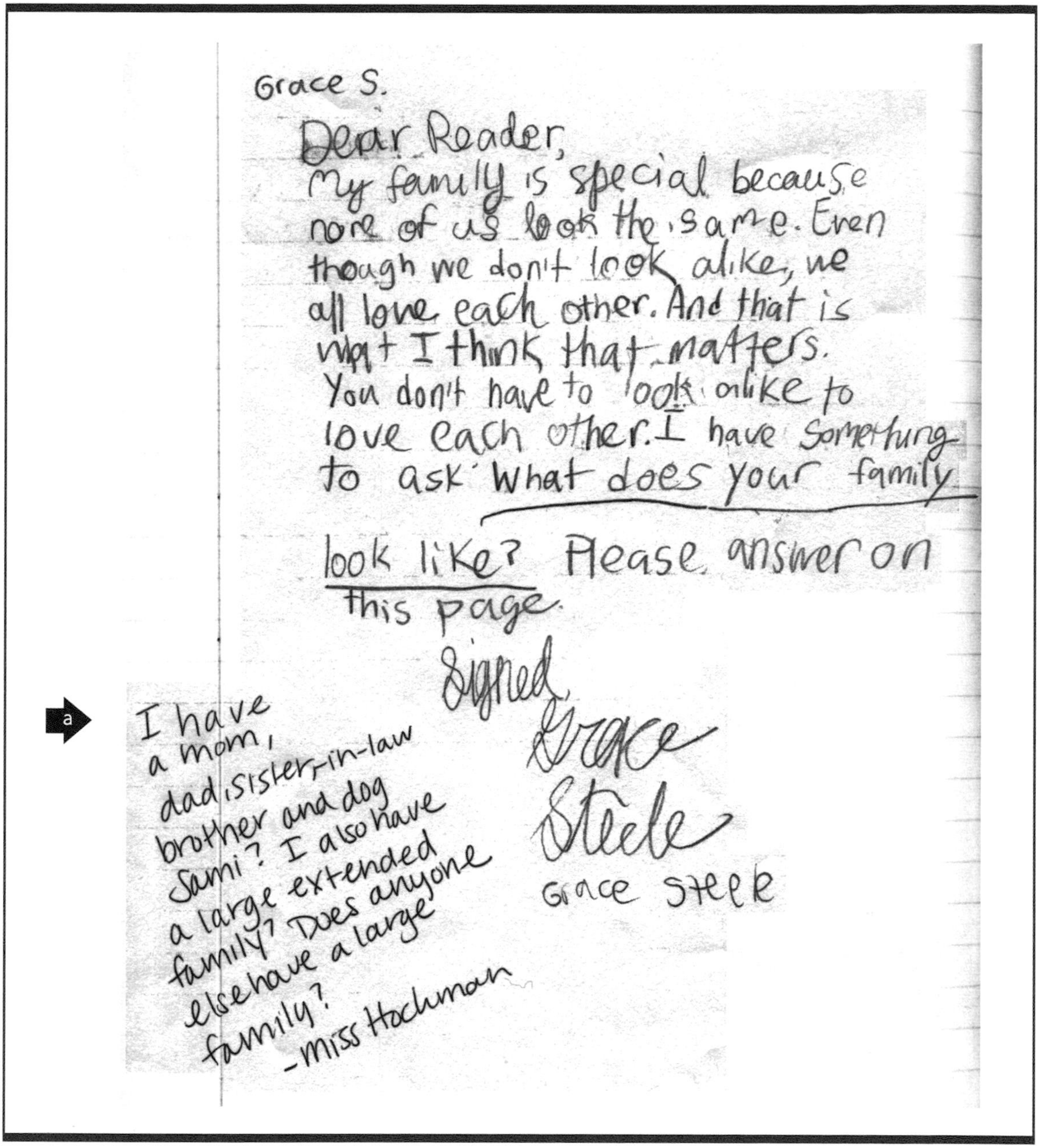

Grace S.

Dear Reader,
My family is special because
none of us look the same. Even
though we don't look alike, we
all love each other. And that is
what I think that matters.
You don't have to look alike to
love each other. I have something
to ask what does your family

look like? Please answer on
this page.
Signed,
Grace
Steele
Grace Steele

I have
a mom,
dad, sister-in-law
brother and dog
Sami? I also have
a large extended
family? Does anyone
else have a large
family?
—Miss Hochman

Grace knows how to keep a conversation going—if you pose a question, you will probably get some answers. Miss Hochman provides one, and then she poses another question for whoever comes into this journal next.

Figure 2.12

a short letter and dropped it in her own box. And the next week, on the desk from which I was supposed to observe, I found a letter addressed to me. Yes, from the student teacher.

We kept corresponding this way throughout the quarter, as well as talking in person and on the phone. Our letters became a separate channel of communication where we could connect and reflect in a special way. And I could see the same thing was happening with her kids, who cheerfully filled each other's mailboxes with friendly, newsy correspondence that the teacher never had to assign.

I started doing some research and learned about a huge variety of classroom mail systems. For middle school kids, Nancie Atwell had already pioneered the use of literature letters between kids and kids, and between the teacher and kids. For this kind of correspondence, most teachers created some kind of shelf—like a mailbox in the back of their classrooms—where class members could mail notes to each other, and pick up letters when their mailbox was full. Many of these teachers set up a rotation where a few kids worked as postmasters each day, delivering mail to people's boxes.

Back in the day, there was a cool program offered by the U.S. Postal Service called "WeeMail." The USPS would provide the materials: paper, envelopes, an address system, and more. They gave you fake mailboxes to place around the school, so students, teachers, staff, and administrators could write to anyone they wanted. Kids from different classrooms, or siblings in the same school, could write to each other. Parents could join the communication also, writing to teachers, their own students, or the cafeteria staff. Kids volunteered for and ran the mail system with adult supervision. Sadly, with all the Post Office's financial woes, funding has now been dropped (maybe FedEx will pick it up?), but the program has still been maintained in some schools.

One "survivor" is Alane Barker, who teaches first grade at St. Andrew's School in Virginia. She has a classroom post office that does a lot.

Figure 2.13

To establish the habit of regular, friendly correspondence, Alane has kids write what she calls "warm and fuzzy" letters to each other, mailing them through the classroom mailbox. Once a regular flow is established, the post office becomes more and more integrated into the work of the room. "I use the mail center as an organizational tool. Each student has an assigned box. Each day they place all the classroom folders they need that day in their box. Later, I write comments on kids' folders individually and place them back into the students' boxes. If I pass out graded papers, students are responsible for putting work in their boxes to take home. Also if a student misses a day, when I pass out work to the class, the absent child's work is placed in their mailbox so that their makeup is waiting on them when they return."

TEACHER-STUDENT FRIENDLY LETTERS

Primary teachers know that kids happily fill us in on their interests and adventures, before we even ask. We often receive notes like shown in Figure 2.14.

Mrs. R.

I am very hot. My pants are muddy. I have a head ach. I had a skirt picked out, but my dad said put the skirt away and put on pants. He is always grumpy in the morning, but this time he was acting wierd. Would you answer? Answer on this.

Dear Ashley,
    It sounds like you had a rough start to your day.
    I'll open another window. Are you too ill to stay at school?
                    Mrs. R.

No. since it has been so quiet, I lost my head-ach. I ♡ my teacher!

Letters give us a private channel through which kids can let us know what's up with them, and we can respond quickly, unobtrusively. Often, just the exchange of notes itself, the human acknowledgment, is helpful or healing. Here, that's exactly what Milwaukee teacher Elise Riepenhoff has done.

Figure 2.14

In the old days, such missives usually arrived folded up on your desk; today, they are just as likely to appear in your email inbox. All these letters give us a clue to how much kids value a one-to-one correspondence with their teachers. The little ones actually reach out for it. So let's reach out to them first. (And this totally goes for teachers of big hulking teenagers, too, so stay tuned.)

How do we structure the exchange of friendly letters? They can just be loose and travel through a classroom mail system. Or you can have kids keep them together in a journal or notebook. They can be occasional, or they can be written on a regular schedule. If you are teaching a self-contained elementary grade and have a small class, you can do daily short exchanges with each kid. Marny's teacher, in early third grade, offers a few tidbits about her own life, as Marny shares hers in Figure 2.15.

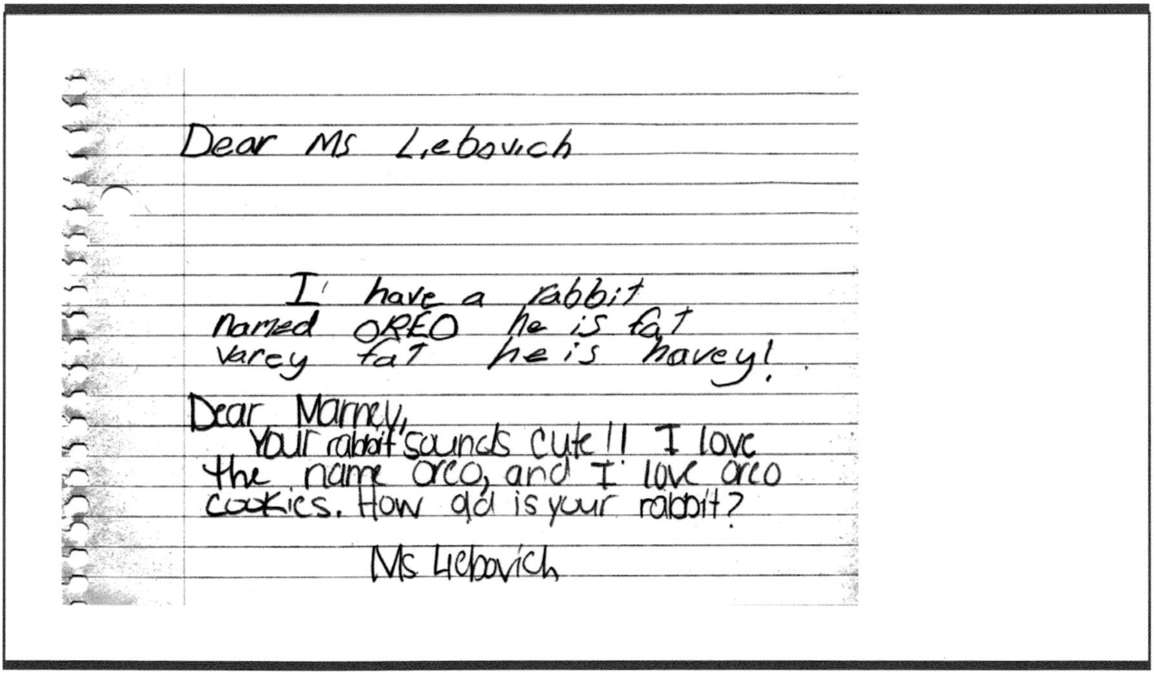
Dear Ms Liebovich

I have a rabbit named OREO he is fat varey fat he is havey!

Dear Marney,
Your rabbit sounds cute!! I love the name oreo, and I love oreo cookies. How old is your rabbit?
Ms Liebovich

Figure 2.15 (continued)

Figure 2.15 (continued)

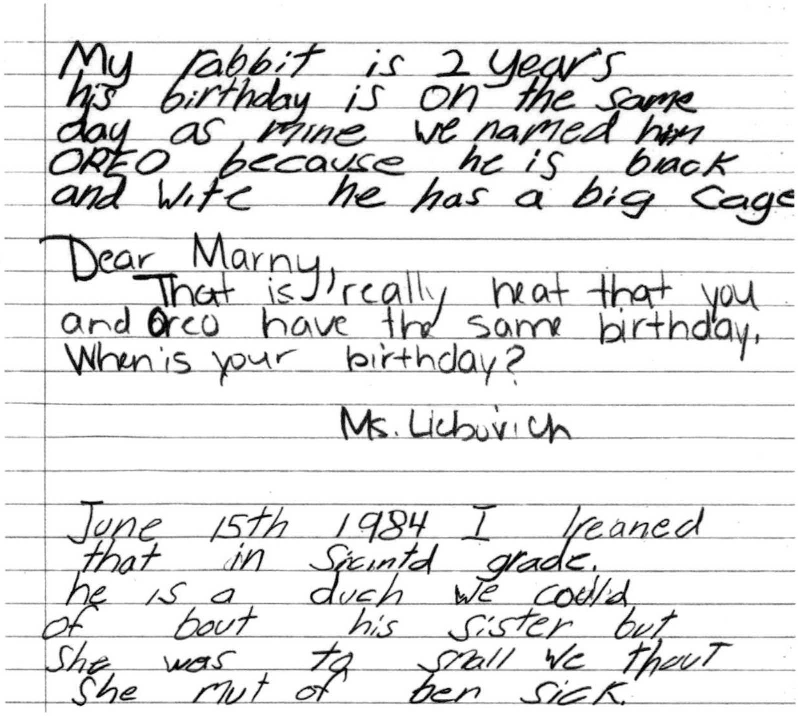

My rabbit is 2 years
his birthday is on the same
day as mine we named him
OREO because he is black
and wite he has a big cage

a Dear Marny,
That is really neat that you
and Oreo have the same birthday,
When is your birthday?

Ms. Lichovich

June 15th 1984 I leaned
that in Sicintd grade.
he is a duch We could
of bout his sister but
She was ta small We thouT
She rlut of ben sick.

He is a Dutch. We could
have bought his sister
but she was too small.
We thought she might
have been sick.

a Teachers sustain written conversations with kids by asking questions (and
follow-up questions) about their out-of-school life and interests.

Figure 2.15

A few months later, while learning cursive, Marny jives with her student
teacher (see Figure 2.16).

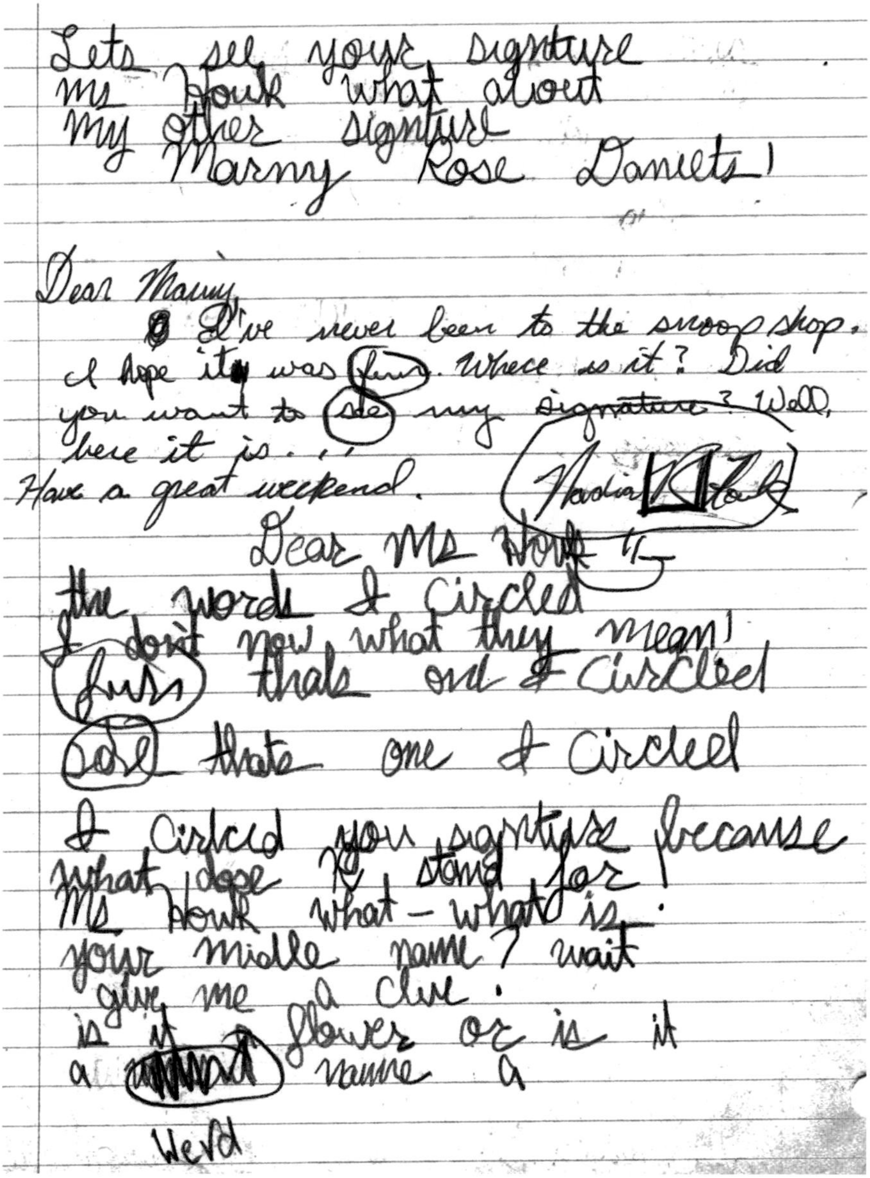

Lets see your signture
Ms Houk what about
My other signture
Marny Rose Daniels!

Dear Marny,
I've never been to the snoop shop. I hope it was fun. Where is it? Did you want to see my signature? Well, here it is...
Have a great weekend. Nadia K Houk

Dear Ms Houk!
the words I circled
I dont now what they mean!
fun thats one I circled
see thats one I circled
I circled you signtue because
what does K stand for!
Ms Houk what-what is
your midle name? wait
give me a clue.
is it a flower or is it
a weird name a
Werd

The words I circled I don't know what they mean! "Fun" that's one I circled. "She" that's one I circled. I circled your signature because what does K stand for? Ms Houk what is your middle name? Wait, give me a clue. Is it a flower or Is It a weird name, a rare name?

a — Marny must feel pretty comfortable, since she is now marking what she judges to be penmanship errors in the teacher's previous letter.

Figure 2.16 (continued)

Figure 2.16 (continued)

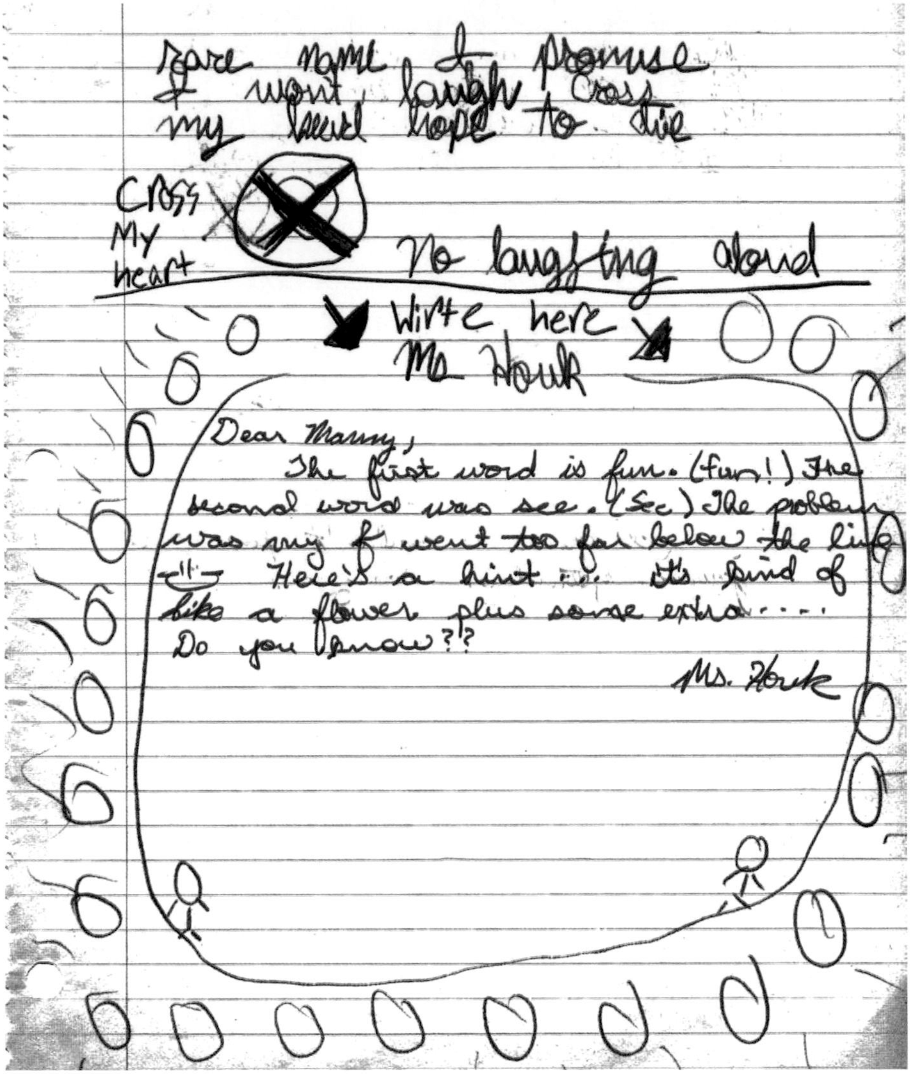

b

your name I promise
I wont laugh Cross
my heart hope to die

Cross
My
heart — No laughing aloud

Write here
Ms. Houk

Dear Marny,
   The first word is fun. (fun!) The
second word was see. (See.) The problem
was my f went too far below the line
↳ Here's a hint ↖ It's kind of
like a flower plus some extra...
Do you know???

                              Ms. Houk

b   Now Marny is trying to pry Ms. Houk's middle name out of her, promising not   Figure 2.16
    to laugh aloud.

The playfulness in these letters, and Ms. Houk's good humor as the student digs for more personal information, strikes just the tone we look for in these exchanges.

In her sixth-grade class in Santa Fe, Joyce Sanchez uses read-alouds to spark friendly letters between herself and the kids. Here, she chats with Jesus about a book called *The Wednesday Surprise*, the story of a 7-year-old girl who secretly teaches her illiterate immigrant grandmother how to read. The topic hits close to home.

> Dear, Ms. Sanchez
> I realy like the pictures in the book
> I was suprised to know that the
> Grandma couldn't read.
> What part, of the story did you like?
> tell me
> your friend, Jesus
>
> Dear Jesus,
>   I was suprised too! I think
> that the Grandma was really brave
> to learn how to read. It reminded
> of me of uncle + aunt who did not learn
> to read until they were in their 60's,
> They went to school to learn. I
> really liked the book.
> Always,
>   Ms. Sanchez

Figure 2.17 (continued)

Figure 2.17 (continued)

Dear Ms, Sanchez
  My Grandma knows how to read
But My Grandpa doesn not know how
to read because he is always sleeping
or watching t.v. I like to go vist
my Grandma because she read
to me.
your friend, Jesus

Dear Jesus,
    I bet your grandma is
a good reader. I wish that
My grandma was still alive. You
are so lucky to have her. I bet
she's a good cook too!
Your friend,
    Ms. Sánchez

a   Joyce is wonderful at kid correspondence because she always shares
     something real of herself and always ends on an affirmative note.

Figure 2.17

In high school, our friend and sometime co-author Nancy Steineke initiates get-to-know-you conversations with her sophomores. Here's a sample of her notes from later in the fall, after she already has some information about each student.

Dear Steve,

Where do you find room for a punching bag *and* a speed bag? They have both of these at one of the gyms I go to. They're located right next to the running track, so I watch people punch while I'm running. I've noticed it takes some skill and rhythm to keep that speed bag going. Do you box or just use that equipment for part of your conditioning?

Dear Katie,

I was kind of surprised that your friend was grounded, but she could still have all her friends over. . . . It was different in my youth, I guess! So which of our local bands are you hearing, and where do they play? That must be fun to hang out with the performers. Do you play any instruments yourself? I could really picture you as a drummer!

Dear Mike,

Yes, I have eaten at some of the restaurants on West Randolph. One of my favorites is Avec, which is about two blocks west of Sushi Wabi. Do you like sushi? I love it but my husband hates it. My favorites are sashimi and BBQ eel roll. What do you eat at Sushi Wabi?

Note the intentional underlying formula Nancy is using here: Find something that you and the student share and build on it, asking follow-up questions and sharing your own connections.

"Respond sparingly on a schedule you can sustain. You needn't answer each student individually every time. When you are swamped, you can write a whole-class response."

- If you do these kinds of newsy letters, respond sparingly on a schedule you can sustain. You needn't answer each student individually every time. When you are swamped, you can write a whole-class response to a set of notes. The key is to mention or respond to one thing about each person's note as you write:

> Dear Sixth Period,
>
> Thanks for all your notes on Friday. I really enjoyed reading them. Looks like Joe, Jessica, and Shannon all saw the new *Predator* movie—and loved it. Gak! Too scary for me! Congrats go out to Martina and Sasha for their volleyball exploits last Tuesday. Go Thunder! A lot of people said they were stressed about the state test coming up next week, so let me say a few words about that. . . .

Elaine: I have my own way of initiating friendly letters with my students. After my years in high school, these days I teach basic writing at Santa Fe Community College. I mentioned earlier that when I moved to New Mexico, I bought a big metal mailbox, and a kids' art club at a nearby elementary school decorated it for me.

I drag my mailbox to my classes every day, along with odds and ends of colorful paper, markers, and stationery. I plunk the mailbox in the front of the room where it is available for anyone to drop a note or letter they may have brought (once the pump is primed, people really do remember to bring notes for class-mates). I bring my own letters responding to their writing in the mailbox, so in each class we need to designate a mail delivery person to pass out the mail. The flag is up!

During free moments, students are invited to write addressed notes and put them in the mailbox. (Of course, early in the year we talk school-appropriate letter-writing content and language.) Then in the middle of class, at break, the

Figure 2.18

mail carrier passes out the mail. Smiles appear on faces, ha-has are heard, and glances are exchanged. Students can then write responses during free moments or wait to deliver a letter back the next day. In this way, students get to know each other and learn to work together better. I, too, get to know them better through the letters to me. Then, just like Don Graves advised, I become a better teacher to each student.

As the kids get older, they might be a bit dubious about whether teachers are serious about initiating a correspondence. Sara Ahmed's sixth graders were skeptical about this teacher-kid letter stuff (see Figure 2.19).

KID-TO-KID FRIENDLY LETTERS

There are only so many letters we teachers can physically write, and we are totally outnumbered by the kids! The big goal is to get them writing to *each*

"There are only so many letters we teachers can physically write, and we are totally outnumbered by the kids! The big goal is to get them writing to each other."

Jack:	Wait, we can ask you questions?
Sara:	Totally. I will answer back as best as I can, or I'll tell you I have no idea what you are talking about.
Nathan:	So, you actually write us back!?
Sara:	Yes! Wouldn't you love a response to a letter you wrote to someone?
Nathan:	That is so cool!
Anthony:	Whoa, that is really hard for you to write all those.
Sara:	Yep! But it's fun to read all about you dudes.

Figure 2.19

other. So we waste no time setting them up. Here are two 5-year-olds getting acquainted through note-passing. Janais asks a series of friendly questions, which Conrad answers right inside Janais's notes (see Figure 2.20).

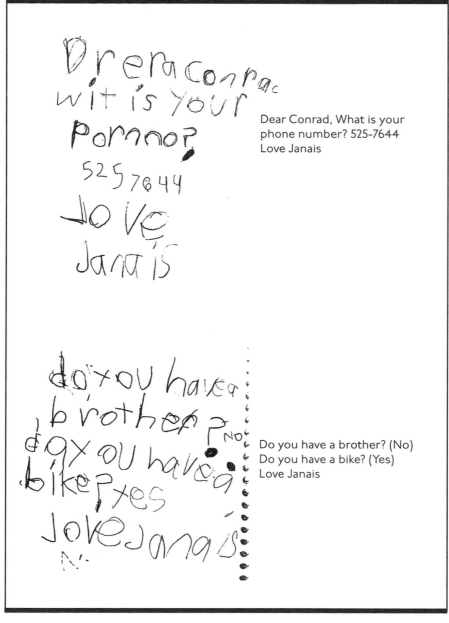

Dear Conrad, What is your
phone number? 525-7644
Love Janais

Do you have a brother? (No)
Do you have a bike? (Yes)
Love Janais

Figure 2.20

Here are a couple more kindergarteners getting acqainted with letters.

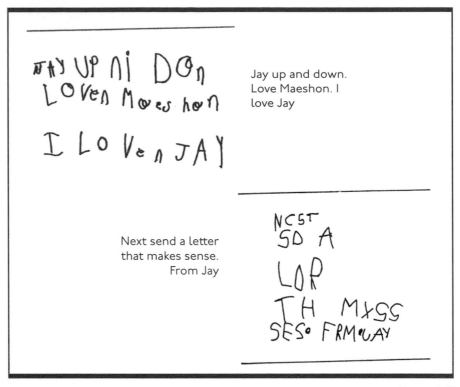

Jay up and down.
Love Maeshon. I
love Jay

Next send a letter
that makes sense.
From Jay

Figure 2.21

Smokey: Last September I visited a school in Oregon and gave a short workshop on written conversation for the whole staff. Then I went off to work with the third-grade team. Unbeknownst to me at the time, the English Language Learners (ELL) teacher marched off down the hall to give it a try with his kids. He paired the students up and gave them the topic to "write about something you are afraid of" (definitely not the first-time prompt I would have recommended). An hour later, he came back down the hall to show me a handful of written results. "These kids have been in school for 20 days," he said, "and they just expressed more about themselves in this writing than I have learned about them all year." He reasoned that the time to think, write carefully, and share with just one other person reduced these language learners' anxiety just enough for them to take a risk and really connect. One especially poignant exchange occcurred between a Mexican boy and a German girl (see Figure 2.22).

Dear Ursla,

I'm afraid to move back to texas. because in texas there is a lot of kids' that make me go to the hostpital, make me bruses, and make me bleed allot some times' I cry

Your friend,

Jose

Dear jose

Im to afride of that beckose I now how that is. In germeny it's the same like in Texas. Kids bet you up and make you bled, and you have to go to the hospital or to the Dogtor and afrl body wil mis you to mi! that's why wie mis you to mi! that's way wie will stay all togesser!!! ☺

Your friend,

Ursula

Figure 2.22

These two children have made an alliance that hopefully will support them all year long.

Once we create the norm of friendly letter-writing in our classrooms, kids find their own business to address. Here, two fourth graders were preparing to give their first joint report of the year.

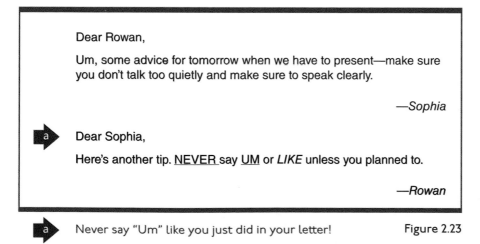

Dear Rowan,

Um, some advice for tomorrow when we have to present—make sure you don't talk too quietly and make sure to speak clearly.

—Sophia

Dear Sophia,

Here's another tip. <u>NEVER</u> say <u>UM</u> or *LIKE* unless you planned to.

—Rowan

Never say "Um" like you just did in your letter!

Figure 2.23

When we see unintended humor, we are allowed to laugh.

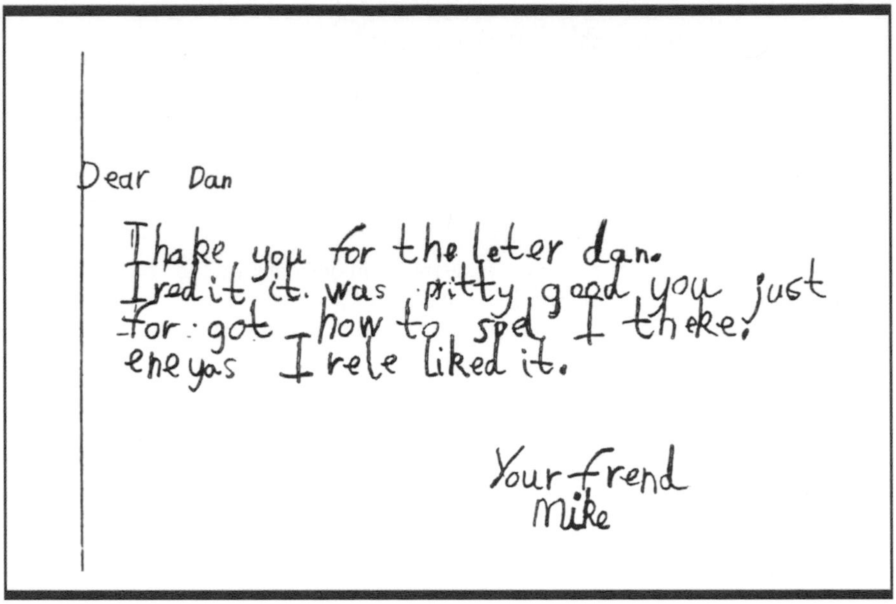

Dear Dan

Thake you for the leter dan.
I rad it it was pitty good you just
for got how to sped I there.
ene yas I rele liked it.

Your frend
Mike

Figure 2.24

MULTI-AGE FRIENDLY LETTERS

There's a special vibration, and often a unique bond inside a school building, when older kids correspond with younger ones. This definitely goes for freshman-senior matchups, as well as primary-intermediate pairings.

At Salazar Elementary School near our home, first-grade teacher Jessica Gonzalez and sixth-grade teacher Joyce Sanchez pair their kids up with writing buddies to exchange letters all year long. In September, before the first graders can really write much, the partners sit side by side, and the big kid does a lot of coaching and scribing. A couple of months later, the 6-year-olds can compose and "mail" their letters to the sixth graders' distant den in the far corner of the school.

Here, big sixth grader Raquel is just getting acquainted with Amanda.

Dear Amanda   Raquel
How's your day been?
what are you doing today?
my day is great

Dear Do you like dukc.

Yes and swans too
I like Swans because there fethers
and puppys.

Raquel   Do you like
    Dukc cakc.

Dear Amanda No if they add duk on it   yuck if
if the don't and dick yes I like it o   they
do you like birds   add
I have 2 birds   duck
a blue one her name is Cloud
and a yellow one his name is Sunshine

Do you ride the bus.

Yes I do
And It's boring.

 Raquel generously offers a nice list of questions to give her new buddy a way to get started.

 But disingenuous provocateur Amanda has a topic ready to go. Do you like ducks?

How about duck *cake*?

Raquel is ready with a rhyming riposte: Yuck if they add duck!

Figure 2.25

If this exchange doesn't crack you up, you're in the wrong line of work. Onward to mini memos!

Prompts and Stems for Written Conversations

These generic prompts or discussion starters are useful for a wide array of classroom correspondence. For many, you have to plug in the appropriate curricular topic and adjust the language to fit your students' grade level. Written conversations can cover any curricular topic or learning experience. Students may discuss a concept, a theory, a poem, a historic period, a novel, a science experiment, a play, a film, a series of images, or any other common topic. These conversations can happen before, during, or after a lesson. And remember, to serve all kids, prompts should be read aloud and also posted or projected.

STARTERS

What's your background knowledge or experience about . . . ?

What do you know about . . . so far?

What do you know—or think you know—about . . . ?

What are you confused or uncertain about?

What is your response to, reaction to, or feeling about . . . ?

What does . . . remind you of in your own life? In the world? In other things you have read/seen on TV?

What do you wonder? What questions do you have?

What would you ask the author/historical figure?

What does . . . make you visualize? What pictures or images appear in your head? Any sounds or music?

Draw a picture, diagram, or cartoon to show your thinking.

What's really important here? What matters most? What's unimportant? How can you tell?

What can you infer from the text/experience?

I was surprised to learn . . .

I was wrong to think . . .

I wonder why . . .

I still don't know/understand . . .

I found it interesting that . . .

It seems especially important that . . .

What are some important "clues"?

What do you think will happen next? How do you know?

With your partner, develop several discussion questions that would help us dig deeper into this topic.

FOLLOW-UPS

What in the text/story/experience made you think that?

Show us where in the book you got that idea.

Can you explain that more?

Are you saying that . . . ?

But what about . . . ?

Take a stand.

What would you claim or argue?

What's the strongest evidence?

What's the weakest evidence?

What other evidence could strengthen your case?

If others were disputing your point of view, what could they say?

PROVOCATIONS

How many sides are there to this story?

Which side are you on? Why?

What's another way to look at this?

Who saw it a different way?

Who disagrees with that?

What's your evidence for . . . ?

I don't see any proof that . . .

Which poem/story/novel/report/article/website is better, and why?

What are the different points of view in your group?

In this text, who benefits from the way things are?

What would the world be like if everyone acted this way?

REFLECTIONS

What's the most important thing we learned today, and why?

What was the most interesting part of today's class?

Take us through today's lesson step by step.

Of all the things we're studying, what is the hardest for you, and why?

What do you predict we will be studying next? What do we need to know to move ahead?

If you were going to explain today's lesson to someone who's not in our class, what would you say?

What are your goals for this course/month/week?

What skills are you going to work at improving?

How are you coming along with the goals you have set for yourself?

How is your group project coming along?

What social skills do you and your partner/group need to work on? What action could you take?

Dear Reader,

At some point, many of us have used super-short writing activities like "exit slips" or "admit slips" to stimulate or capture kids' thinking, right? These quick-writes are often implicitly letters from student to teacher, but we don't usually exploit their full, interactive potential—or their curricular range. In this chapter, we reframe these mini memos as a family of letters that can provide you with an "extreme classroom makeover," two minutes at a time.

Smokey and Elaine

DEFINITION: Mini memos are super-short letters that help transfer thinking and responsibility to students. Imagine a note that fits on a 3 × 5 index card—a tool we very often use for these communiques. Typically, these notes get passed around from student to student, accumulating multiple responses and then provoking whole-class discussions. Compared to the other variations coming up in the next three chapters, mini memos are less concerned with initiating a small-group conversation than with feeding useful ideas into the whole class. This category pulls together several closely related short-writes that many teachers already use, but shows how their value is enhanced when they are done in *explicit letter form*.

"Mini memos are less concerned with initiating a small-group conversation than with feeding useful ideas into the whole class."

VARIATIONS:

- Morning Message
- Start-Up Notes
- Admit Notes
- Writing Breaks
- Exit Notes

ORIGINS: This family of letters goes back to the 1970s and early 1980s, when pioneers like James Britton, Peter Elbow, and Toby Fulwiler showed that short, in-class writing activities could help students to learn and remember subject matter content. The fundamental insight was that there are two main kinds of writing: formal public writing and writing to learn.

WRITING TO LEARN	PUBLIC WRITING
Short	Substantial
Spontaneous	Planned
Exploratory	Authoritative
Informal	Conventional
Personal	Audience-centered
One draft	Multiple drafts
Unedited	Edited
Ungraded	Assessable

While K–12 schools and colleges had always given attention to extended but infrequent public writing assignments (like term papers, critical essays, and research reports), the value of nonstop, day-in-day-out practice with shorter writings had been overlooked. Redressing this imbalance, a writing to learn movement began mainly in colleges, and then spread to the secondary and elementary schools through the National Writing Project.

QUICK LOOK:

Exit Notes

In Michele's Timble's fourth-grade classroom, the kids are meeting in literature circles, small, peer-led reading discussion groups. Just as in adult book clubs, each four-member group has chosen its own title to read and has made a reading calendar including group meetings after every few chapters. When lit circles gather on those appointed days, the kids are fully responsible for bringing along good, meaty discussion topics from the story.

Today, most groups are about halfway through their chosen books, including some school-themed favorites like *Frindle, No Talking, Lunch Money,* and *The Report Card.* As the meetings come to a close, Michele says, "All right, guys, we're almost out of time for meeting, so please wrap up in one minute." As kids' conversations wind down, Michele places a stack of brightly colored 4 × 6 index cards on each group's table.

"Now we are going to take some time to reflect on your discussions today. Before we started our book clubs, we worked on some specific discussion skills that are important, no matter what the book is, right? Here's the chart we made a couple of weeks ago (she flips back to an anchor chart made before the book clubs were formed). So, we talked about being respectful, including everyone, building on other people's ideas, using evidence from the text, and all these other things. Everybody remember this list of discussion skills? OK.

"So right now I'm going to have you write me an exit note telling me how your group did today in using the social skills of small-group discussion. Please give me specific examples of what happened. I'll give you about three minutes.

Happy writing, everyone." Shortly, Michele collects a stack of exit notes including these comments:

Dear Ms. Timble,

Our meeting went great when we were talking about the war and why the grandma was in pain. We did some piggybacking about it too. The only problem was that we talk over each other but we fixed it up a bit. We tried to take turns too!

Elizabeth

Here's a hint of a common problem. But let's remember, if you visit most adult book groups, you will see *lots* of interrupting.

Dear Ms. Timble,

I thought that we got a lot of key points in the book! We all contributed and almost never got off topic. First, when I asked how everybody liked the book, Raleigh made a good point that we were almost halfway done and nothing big has happened. We all stared talking about that. All the little things that might lead to something big. Olivia shared her feelings about the book and then shared text evidence. Then Ted pointed out another text evidence. Then I shared my opinion and looked something else up in the book. We all agreed and rapped it up. It was a great discussion!

Anna

 A pretty good insight—most books have plenty of action and plot turns by this point.

Figure 3.1 (continued)

 We like it when kids use this kind of thinking language, but we also want to check and see what the evidence is.

Figure 3.1 (continued)

Dear Ms. Timble,

Me and Emma brought up the main topic about our discussion. We were taking turns but a little trouble with interrupting. We had a great discussion and stayed on topic the whole time! We were retelling the book really good!

Love, Bryce

Dear Ms. Timble,

Katy brought up very good points about why she was getting bad grades and we all were talking and piggybacking and Miles also brought up a good point a bout her plan to purposely get bad grades. And Lilly said "Well I think that she was trying to prove a point" and I piggybacked and said because she wanted to stop the kids from putting themselves into groups.

—Sinserly, Olivia

---

d Retelling is not the same as discussing; Michele checks to make sure these kids are going beyond factual recall.

Figure 3.1

e Meaning, stop the kids from forming cliques.

Tonight, at home, Michele will scan the stack of exits, use them to assess how her students' group work is going, and plan her teaching for tomorrow. While kids are generally reporting energetic and on-task discussions, there's one strand of concern: people interrupting or talking over each other. So first thing the next morning, Michele will look at the kids and say, "While I was reading your exit notes last night, I heard a lot of good things about how your book club meetings were going." To mark those accomplishments, she'll read a few celebratory examples from kids' cards. And then she'll say, "I also noticed that several groups were having a common problem," and read aloud a couple of notes about interruptions. "Let's talk about how we can fix that," Michelle will say, flipping to a fresh sheet of chart paper. "Let's make a list of things we can do to stop interrupting each other in our book clubs."

LAUNCHING LESSON:

Admit Notes

High school teacher Wayne Mraz doesn't begin today's U.S government class by lecturing on the constitutional requirements for presidential candidates—though that is one topic coming up. Instead, as homework the night before, he assigned kids to bring in a short "admit note" describing the qualities of their ideal president. These letters aren't addressed to anyone in particular, but once they come through the classroom door (where Wayne bars entry to anyone who hasn't brought their card), they are immediately put to work. Among today's entries were the following:

I think its cool that we have an African American president elected two times in this country. Maybe this proves that we are not such a racist country after all like some people think. I think Obama has done a good job and I wish he could get elected for a third time, like Roosevelt was it?— maybe we could change the constitution?
10/10

It is rae-donkulous that you have to be 35 to be president!! There are plenty of smart younger people who could do the job. But maybe when they wrote the Constitution, 35 was old??
10/10

I want a president who will bring my brother home from Afghanistan. We need to protect our country from crazy terrorists and bombers. But my brother is in the army in Afghanistan right now and you would not believe what those guys are going through out there. He says they are just targets for the Taliban to shoot at and they aren't accomplishing anything.
10/10

Figure 3.2 (continued)

Figure 3.2 (continued)

I think a president should be Honest, futuristic, smart and to Be able to face the facts, about anything he says.

10/10

One who sounds trustful and looks write and is smart enough and one who want to do something about the Earth.
    I think it hard to say who becomes president because they all say things just to win and after they win they dont do it. So I say Dont vote for anyone these are my thoughts.

10/10

These samples show the wide range of responses we typically get with admit notes, and there are several that would serve as great discussion starters. Though the level of thinking (and punctuation) varies widely here, each note has a kernel worth talking about. Because each student made a "good faith effort," everyone received 10 out of 10 possible points.

Figure 3.2

As kids take their seats, Wayne is now holding a deck of kids' thoughts about what makes a good president. He has several good instructional options:

• **Focus on the range of responses**. Shuffle quickly through the deck, reading aloud a few that catch his eye and that reflect the range of responses. Kids will be perked up, waiting to see if their card is read. (If you do this enough times, kids will start crafting their admit notes with an eye toward grabbing your attention.) Now, Wayne can simply segue to his prepared lesson on the presidency and carry on (until the next writing opportunity).

- **Focus on a provocative discussion starter**. Look for a card that can launch a lively conversation. In the last sample in Figure 3.2, Wayne comes across the rather bleak, but perhaps mordant, comment that "they all say things Just to win and after they win they don't do it." He can read this one aloud and ask people for comments, initiating a discussion that lures kids into the topic. As students volunteer responses, Wayne can keep flipping through the deck looking for cards that advance or redirect the conversation. This could go on for two or five minutes depending on how Wayne sees the value of the discussion.

- **Write more and share**. Pass the cards back randomly so everyone receives someone else's admit note. Wayne can instruct the kids to read that card, then flip it over and write a response to the student who wrote side one. Then he calls on a few volunteers to read aloud both sides of their card. If students do this on full-size paper instead of cards, kids can pass them down a row or around a table of seats in one-minute intervals, with each successive person adding to the previous students' comments (a rudimentary write-around; see pages 155–191).

Whatever choice Wayne makes, the important thing is that the kids' work is *getting used in class*. This is not just a homework assignment that lands in the teacher's inbox. Instead, kids' thinking is honored by being put to work. (We know—you're noticing those "10/10s" on the cards, right? Wayne says that if kids make a "good faith effort" to complete one of these quick-think notes, they earn full credit. No 3s, no 7s. All or nothing.)

And don't overlook all the good academic work that's being done with these admit notes. Wayne uses them to do the following:

- Introduce the topic
- Get kids engaged

- Surface background knowledge

- Build curiosity

- Include kids' voices from the get-go

All within a couple of minutes. Now, "covering the curriculum" can commence immediately, with kids actually ready to learn.

MORNING MESSAGE

Purpose: Begin the school day with the teacher and students co-creating a letter that builds anticipation for upcoming learning.

One form of teacher-to-student writing that's already quite common in American elementary classrooms is something called "morning message." Typically, the teacher writes a letter addressed to a class of students on large chart paper, and uses it as part of the opening rituals of the school day. Regie Routman was among the first educators to write about the value of this special correspondence (2004), and another version of morning message is promoted by the admirable organization Responsive Classroom and detailed in several of its books.

At its best, morning message begins with a big blank page (or projection screen), on which the teacher composes a letter "live," right in front of the children. She talks about her writing process as she composes, much as teachers do when offering a reading "think-aloud."

GENERAL INSTRUCTIONS FOR MINI MEMOS

RE: Morning Messages. The teacher composes a note to the whole class, live and on stage. In this special "write-aloud," the teacher may also invite students to offer suggestions as co-creators of the letter. A typical topic in the lower grades is some version of "Dear Class, Here's what we're going to do today." With older kids, teachers may create letters that respond to a text or news event, or are invitations to address a class problem: "We have been talking about sharing materials in our room, but I am still seeing . . ."

The next three types of think notes are written by students within one to three minutes, often on index cards. Then the notes are either

- Read aloud by the teacher

- Discussed

- Passed around the room and discussed or written upon

The goal is to evoke curiosity and build background about the day's curricular goals. The teacher may make a list of the topics raised and show how they connect to the day's lesson.

RE: Start-Up Writes. Written when kids first arrive in class, these notes are designed to help students prepare for the upcoming lesson. This often means the following:

- Surfacing background knowledge

- Evoking questions

- Grappling with puzzling or counterintuitive aspects of the topic

Often the core prompt is "What do you know" or "What do you wonder about . . . ?"

RE: Admit Slips. The topics and uses are basically the same as for start-up writes, but now kids bring these notes with them to class, having prepared them as homework. This saves more class time for interaction around the students' ideas. Teachers need backup plans for kids who show up note-free.

RE: Writing Breaks. Done in the middle of class sessions, these are brief partner exchanges where the subject is the content of the lesson in progress. Writing breaks are explicitly focused on supporting students' here-and-now understanding of content being presented.

The key question is, "What are you understanding/not understanding right now about . . . ?"

RE: Exit Notes. At the end of a class or lesson, students write a note to the teacher in which they talk about their:

- Understanding of the topic of the day

- Questions about it

- Connections to it

Teachers study these writings to plan future teaching, and often begin the following class by reading from or using the previous day's exit notes.

OK, you guys, I'm going to start today's letter with our usual salutation here, so "Dear Inquiring Minds of 406." Good, now somebody remind me, what's the date? Right, the first, of course! So I'll write, "Today is November 1, 2014." Now, what's coming up this week?

Combining his or her own goals for the day with suggestions from the students (and continuously voicing his or her writerly decision making), the teacher completes a whole letter that might turn out like Figure 3.3.

Dear Inquiring Minds of 406,

Today is November 1, 2014. The Learning Fair is only four days away—whoa! We have a lot of work to get ready for the parents and community friends visiting us Friday. The alderman is even coming! She is the person who represents our neighborhood to the mayor.

So let's start the day by gathering in our project groups for a "midcourse correction." We'll use our work plans and calendars to see how we should schedule ourselves over the next couple of days.

We'll follow our usual schedule through lunch. Then Ms. Abrams is coming in at 1:30 to teach us a cool new app called Songify that you can use to make your book reviews into songs. How does that sound? Cool, awesome, neat!

Sounds like a big day, a fun day.

Are you in?

Ms. Fletcher

a Here, the teacher turned to the class and asked, "Does everyone know what an alderman is?" Seeing some puzzled faces, she added the next sentence.

b Here, the teacher asked kids to contribute a few words to describe the afternoon plan.

Figure 3.3

This engaging process displays an adult's writing-as-thinking and product, while simultaneously helping students think ahead to the key activities of the day.

We have been disappointed in recent years to see morning messages more often used for "skill work" on spelling, grammar, or phonics, rather than as real letter-writing. Sometimes teachers will even pepper their own letters with intentional mistakes and ask students to find and correct them. Maybe that's OK as a low-level editing drill, but it doesn't teach anything about composing, and it sure doesn't spark kids' curiosity. One popular methods book even advises teachers to write these messages in advance, to "cut down on the stress of trying to think and write under pressure." Say what? What about the pressure *kids* face when we ask them to write? This is exactly what kids need to see their teachers doing every day: thinking and composing aloud in real "pressured" circumstances!

When incorporated into the opening meeting of a school day, authentic morning messages accomplish several useful things:

- Offer a live demonstration of adult writing strategies

- Set academic purposes for the day

- Invite kids to buy into—and help create—the agenda

- Create community as everyone pitches in and focuses on shaping the message

- Give an opportunity to introduce new or key vocabulary words (e.g., *alderman*) and talk about them

After a morning message has been completed and discussed, some teachers invite kids to stop by the chart and sign in on the bottom. Or they can add a Post-it note to ask or answer a question that was posed or to comment on a subject in the message.

If morning message becomes a regular part of every school day's rituals—or it does for Mondays only, or at the beginning of new units—it also becomes an anchor chart that can be saved, looked back upon, and studied as a piece of class history. "Can anyone remember when we started working on punctuating dialogue? Let's look at our old morning messages and see if we can find it. Oh, here, here it is, October 23."

START-UP NOTES

Purpose: Launch the day or class session by writing someone a note about the currculum topic under study.

Start-up notes and admit notes are essentially the same in purpose and function: launching the day or a class session by writing someone a note about the curriculum topic under study. But there's one big difference: Start-up notes (like

morning messages) are done *in class*, after everyone has arrived. Admit notes are supposed to be written *before class*, often as homework, and then act as a ticket of admission to the class. In other words, kids have to remember to complete and bring an admit note. Or to be blunt, you can count on some kids forgetting theirs, so you need to be ready with Plan B for homework refuseniks. For these reasons, we start by doing in-class writes and move to true admit notes after kids have come to understand and value this kind of writing.

Many teachers start their class day with a "sponge activity," a quiet writing task that's posted when kids walk into the room. Attributed to Madeline Hunter, these solitary tasks are designed to "soak up" kids' random energy during transitions, especially right at the beginning of the class. This stops kids from, uh, what? Greeting each other? Chatting as they settle in? Anyway, we'll concede that this is a plausible idea, potentially enforcing a strong work ethic and high level of productivity.

Unfortunately, most sponges we see are pretty soggy. "If you were a butterfly, how would you feel?" or "Name as many state capitals as you can" or "List three phyla of plants we have studied." Of course, primary-age kids will play along with any crazy assignment teachers come up with, but as kids get a little older, these manufactured topics interest only a few, their purpose is vague, and little curiosity is ignited. The kids recognize this kind of sponge for what it is: busywork unconnected to the curriculum, done out of duty and compliance.

But this valuable seed of an idea—starting the class with a start-up note—can provide an energizing and curriculum-enhancing start to the day if we make it a letter with a real audience and a real purpose. When Colleen Girard's kindergarteners walked into their class one day in October, they saw this written on the board (and she also read it aloud, of course):

Good morning, 102!

We are going to start studying PLANTS today! Look at the books on your tables for a while.

Then, write me a note: What do you wonder about plants or trees? What questions do you have?

At their tables of four, the kids excitedly flip through their bin of nonfiction picture books about plants, trees, flowers, vegetables, and forests. There are pads of sticky notes and lots of markers available.

After they enjoy a few minutes of reading and picture-walking, Ms. Girard invites kids to write her a note about their questions about plants. Some kids write words, some draw, some dictate to Mrs. G or the classroom aide. When they are ready, kids go and post their note on a piece of chart paper at the front of the room. Some of these 5-year-olds haven't used this tool before (if they don't know where the sticky stuff is, it can be pretty hard to adhere the note to a loose piece of chart paper), so there are some funny struggles at the chart. A few of the kids' offerings follow.

Written by children
   Dear Ms G, Why do we need plants?
   Ms G, How do flowrs grow trees?
   To Miss G, Why do plans grow undrwatr?
   I am namd aftr a plat, from Daisy
   What kind of plans eat and snap at flys?

Dictated to an adult
   How do you grab spiked plants?
   How does honey come out of a flower?

Figure 3.4

And, from Marco, came a classic:

Figure 3.5

Colleen was able to reassure Marco that he was not in fact a plant—and this initiated a great conversation about the differences between plants and animals—a perfect way to start the unit.

ADMIT NOTES

Purpose: Kids come to class with prewritten notes about a curricular topic; these writings are then used to spark the day's studies.

Now let's look more closely at the true admit note, where kids bring a mimi memo along with them to class. Up in the Launching Lesson section (pages 76–79), we already gave one pretty good example of what admit notes can look like in high school. But admit notes, drawn or written, work at all grade levels. And, for the younger ones, this is a great first type of homework assignment, something that parents and kids can work on together at home, briefly and pleasantly. No tears, just fun.

Some teachers like to play with the ticket metaphor and issue forms like these for kids to create their admit notes.

Figure 3.6

Here are a couple of admit note samples from a sixth-grade class in suburban Phoenix. On February 21, teacher James Kissling asked the kids to create an admit slip with one key question and one interesting finding from their individual research projects. The next day, these short notes became the basis of small-group meetings where kids shared and discussed their investigations.

THIS TICKET IS GOOD FOR

05321   05321

My question: How many books did she actually write that got published?
I thought that Louisa May Alcott proved that women were good at doing things that men did instead of just doing housework. She proved that by writing so many books + getting them published.

NAME Janessa Hutzer   DATE 2/27/00

For this admit note, kids were asked to share both their research question and some of their key findings.

Figure 3.7

A few weeks later, when kids were reading about the lives of famous scientists, James assigned an admit note telling "one interesting or surprising thing you learned about the scientist you studied."

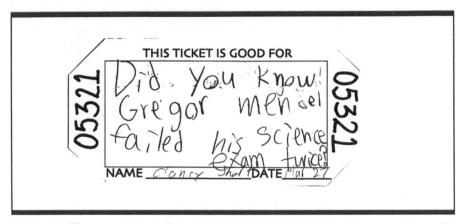

THIS TICKET IS GOOD FOR

05321

Did you know Gregor menc[el] failed his science exam twice?

05321

NAME Clancy Sha[?] DATE Mal 27

The prompt was "Bring in one interesting or surprising fact from your research on famous scientists." Class then began with a sharing of these interesting tidbits.

Figure 3.8

Notes like this one laid the foundation for a discussion about how some famous scientists actually didn't do well in school. Maybe some geniuses were "late bloomers," the kids speculated.

In Elaine's college English classes, she often asks students to bring admit notes in the form of suggested discussion questions for the story, novel, poem, or play they have read the night before. The students quoted next had read *The Miracle Life of Edgar Mint* by Brady Udall, and brought these admit slips to spark the morning's discussion.

> I would want to talk about the things that happened in the first paragraph—"the left postal jeep tire ground my tiny head into the gravel of the San Carlos Apache Reservation."

> On p. 117 in the second paragraph the mailman took his shirt and his pants off to put on the boy's head and I admire his action.

> When the mailman screamed, why didn't she look for her son? I wonder why she just sat there all day.

Let's talk about his impression of how his life would go with his drunken Mom and a crazy witch grandma.

I think the teachers should have stepped in or that they should have noticed the treatment he was getting from the bullies.

I didn't like how the boy had to somehow change his ways to fit in with the bullies or anyone else for that matter, just because he wasn't afraid to be who he was. No one should ever have to be ashamed of what they are and even if he were to somehow change, which he couldn't, why would he want to hang around the people that bullied him? This infuriates me.

Edgar had a flashback of when he was born and he thought he saw the person who used his mother for sex. Was he right?

Grandma Paul was praying that Edgar would be resurrected from the dead, but I think he was by her side all this time.

There are plenty of ideas here to ignite a conversation about the story. Another reminder that we can begin class discussions with kids' questions and connections. And when students miss key issues, we can jump right in with any topics they've neglected.

Do students really need a teacher peppering them with questions when they can bring topics like these to class in admit notes? Who's taking responsibility, doing the work, the thinking, now?

WRITING BREAKS

Purpose: Help students collect and synthesize their thoughts during pauses in teacher presentations.

As kids move up through the grades, one of the worsening problems is that

© Ocean/Corbis.

we teachers talk too much. Guilty, but honest, we can't help it! At some level, we do recognize that students are sitting through our presentations, taking superficial notes at best and sleeping at worst.

So we have to make time and provide a structure for kids to actively engage with the valuable ideas we are sharing. And the beauty is, we can do that two minutes at a time. All we have to do is stop—and let the kids use writing to get their thinking down. That's why this activity is sometimes called "stop and write."

Want to try the two-minute lecture makeover? Set your class up in pairs, where everyone has a writing buddy seated near them, with blank sheets of paper ready to go. Look for natural breaks in the lesson during which you can stop and invite partners to write to each other "what I understand/don't understand, right now." You can just try it once in the middle of a class, but stopping every seven or eight minutes is optimal.

In Al Gridley's biology class, the day's lesson is about *ionizing radiation,* a fairly complex concept, and one that's subject to many misconceptions. So after the first 10 minutes of his lecture, Kent pauses and asks kid partners to write each other 1-minute notes. Melly and Rose work hard to clarify their understanding.

You may recognize these writing breaks as the written equivalent of the "pair shares" or "turn and talks" we use in our classrooms all the time. Knowing as we do that peer conversation enhances both comprehension and achievement (Allington, 2012), we want to consistently provide for both kinds of peer talk, written and spoken. And as we have also noted before, the written version of these conversations provides equal "airtime" to both participants, rules out side conversations, invites more thoughtful ideas, and can be collected and assessed by teachers.

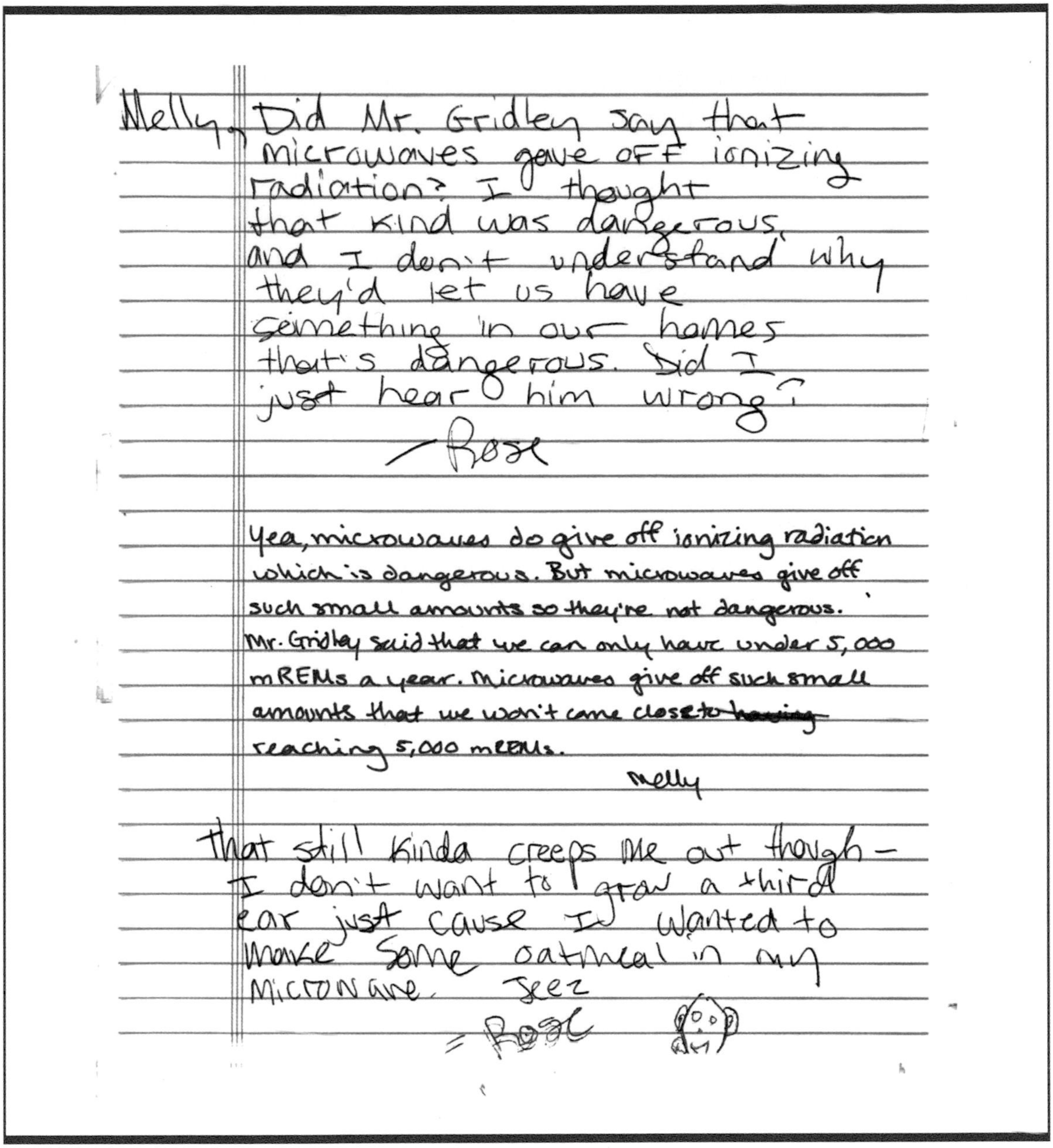

Melly, Did Mr. Gridley say that microwaves gave off ionizing radiation? I thought that kind was dangerous, and I don't understand why they'd let us have something in our homes that's dangerous. Did I just hear him wrong?

— Rose

Yea, microwaves do give off ionizing radiation which is dangerous. But microwaves give off such small amounts so they're not dangerous. Mr. Gridley said that we can only have under 5,000 mREMs a year. microwaves give off such small amounts that we won't come close to ~~having~~ reaching 5,000 mREMs.

Melly

That still kinda creeps me out though — I don't want to grow a third ear just cause I wanted to make some oatmeal in my microwave. Jeez

— Rose

This is one of two sheets that passed between the girls during their quick writing break. When the kids shared their thinking aloud, Al was able to correct their misconception; while microwave ovens do not give off "officially" ionizing radiation, they may still have some damaging effects, according to recent studies.

Figure 3.9

EXIT NOTES

Purpose: At the end of a class session, students reflect on the day's learning and then hand their thoughts to the teacher.

In a way, exit slips can be the easiest mini memo variety to start with. You just save the last two or three minutes of class and give students a prompt that helps them reflect on or synthesize their learning for the day. You can ask them to write you a note telling:

What's the most important thing we learned today, and why?

Of all the things we're studying, what is the hardest for you, and why?

What do you predict we will be studying next? What do we need to know to move ahead?

If you were going to explain today's lesson to someone who's not in our class, what would you say?

In Jim Olsen's math class in Duluth, Minnesota, all kids are matched with a partner for various mini memos throughout the session. Each day, at the end of class, Jim asks the pairs to write an exit note, a reflection on the day's learning. Today, because they have been studying "open figures," the prompt is

Discuss with your math buddy: How could an open figure become a problem in real life?

Jim gives kids just about 45 seconds to jot an initial note, then tells them to swap, read, and respond. Another 45 seconds to answer, and then one more turn to finish the conversation.

Matt: OK so I remember this is a multi-sided figure where one part of it is open. So it could be like a fence that doesn't completely surround a herd of sheep, and then one could get out. Or cows or whatever animal.

Chris: Good idea, ba-ba, so long sheep! Mr Olsen said an OF was a polygon that's not completely closed up, so you would have an open end somewhere. Would that be like if the bottom dropped out of your gas tank, because it rusted?

Matt: Dude, I don't think a gas tank is a "figure." Something like more two dimensional? It's supposed to be a shape with any number of sides, like a triangle or a rectangle or whatever, but one side of it is not connected. Like if they left a door open at the Pentagon in DC? Or when that plane took out one wall there on 9-11? Yuk, bad example, sorry.

So how do teachers *use* exit slips like these? Of course, you collect them as kids file out the door or move on to the next activity. Then, when time permits, you read through the notes *diagnostically*, looking to gauge kids' level of understanding of the day's content. If the notes suggest that the lesson flopped—that many students didn't grasp the concept of an open figure, then you know you need to reteach the lesson.

> *"Read through the notes* diagnostically, *looking to gauge kids' level of understanding of the day's content."*

So perhaps you arrive the next day with a few notes picked out and start the class saying something like "When I was reading through your exit notes last night, I noticed a lot of people saying things like . . . " Then you read aloud from a few of the notes indicating confusion or uncertainty about the subject (no names, if incriminating). Then you go ahead and reteach open figures, possibly using some of the other kids' good examples (e.g., sheep in a pen). Much as with start-ups and admit slips, you are using the notes to advance the work of the class. We acknowledge the kids' efforts by using their own language and ideas to build better understanding.

Another classic version of exit slips is having students process specific class activities, especially ones that are new or complex.

Smokey: When I was teaching some high school demonstration lessons in Arkansas, I asked the kids to comment on three different activities they had tried during the class: viewing a series of images of child labor around the world; doing a stand-up mingling activity in which every student quickly exchanged ideas with eight different partners; and a written conversation much like the ones in this book. Some of the exit slips from that lesson follow.

In the mingle, each kid was given just one sentence from the article he or she would later read. The students had to walk around comparing sentences with other kids, one at a time, trying to figure out from everyone's different sentences what the article would be about. We call this a "quotation mingle."

For shy kids like this young lady, quiet writing time followed by the exchange of letters with classmates is a rare chance to "have our conversation" and "share our thoughts."

Figure 3.10 (continued)

Figure 3.10 (continued)

> **C** ➤ We looked at Some Pictures, read an interesting story about a kid going to war, mingled with each other (cool), had a disscussion about PTSD, which gave me a better understanding of the topic. I would be excited if we did more things like this.

C ➤ When he says we "had a discussion," he is referring to the written conversation. This lesson showed how teachers can set up six or eight different activities during a middle or high school class period, instead of one long presentation. The kids uniformly liked the quick pace and variety. With the right structures in place, even our most "bored" teenagers are ready to work hard and do well.

Figure 3.10

While exit slips like these help us to assess our teaching day by day, they also give us the broader reminder that it's always smart to actually ask the kids, instead of guessing how things seem to them.

Mini memos can have maxi impact. They allow you to "stick your toe in the water" of written conversation without committing large chunks of class time or fearing the kids' ranging off topic. Once they have gained confidence with this family of quick-writes, many teachers will use two, three, or four of these techniques *every day* to keep students active, responsible, and thinking. That's why we often call mini memos "The Two-Minute Classroom Makeover."

© Getty Images.

Is There Time for This?

As we enjoy all these teacher and kid letters, you might be thinking, "Hey, if I asked all my students to write me a letter about their reading or some other class activity, I could be saddling myself with hours of work responding to them all!" Well, you're right—it could happen.

Smokey: When I first started using dialogue journals (for the record, in 1970), I asked all 145 of my high school seniors to write me notes, and had them all due Friday. You can imagine the Lost Weekend that followed this unwise assignment. After some surprisingly extensive additional misjudgments, I learned that I could manage to write a thoughtful, patient, openhearted, unrushed letter to just five kids a day. And on that schedule, I could get to one class section per week, which meant that every kid got a letter from me about every five weeks, or eight times a year. I felt that this schedule was extremely valuable to both me and the kids; I was able to hold regular written conferences with every kid, and we learned plenty about each other as we corresponded.

Elaine: I run the same risk when I commit to writing dialogue journals with my students. I usually start the year by inviting them to share their autobiographies as readers and writers. I get a whole big stack of these letters, which I love because I get to know the students so much better as people. It's a strong basis for building the class community. Then I write each student a response, usually handwritten on stationery (sometimes, when my hand wears out, I do resort to the computer). I write in the friendly letter form, always starting with "Dear Antonio" or "Dear Red Horse." I have to say that around the middle of this stack, I have to do some deep breathing. At that point, I decide to respond to the other half of the papers tomorrow!

While one-to-one letters between teachers and students can be extremely powerful, they can and should be used sparingly and strategically. We never want writing to our kids to become a burden or a hassle to us; our impatience will shine right through if we tackle too much. Remember, we can always respond with one whole-class letter that mentions everyone, and make copies for all.

Dear 102,

Thanks for all your awesome notes! So many of you wrote about our trip to the recycling center. Wendy, Jose, and June thought the huge trash masher was the coolest—me too! Randy was surprised to find that our bus driver was Mrs. Wright, just like in every morning coming to school. Elise and Tom thought that our guide, Ms. Spychalski, was really knowledgeable. Naomi made a good point—we should have asked what kind of schooling you need to get a job like hers. We have to write a thank-you letter anyway, so we should be sure to ask her about that . . .

In this way, we are still keeping up our end of the conversational bargain, without writing 30 separate notes. And in tech-enabled classrooms, we can post our individual or whole-class letters on our Edmodo page or whatever web space the school supports, thus saving both time and trees. And we must always remember that the *most* important, day-to-day, knowledge-building written conversations are not with us, but between kid and kid!

Dear Reader,

Now we move into the yearlong uses of written discussions for teaching the curriculum. In this chapter, we start simple and straightforward, with written conversations between just two people. This natural (and accountable) letter-writing structure has time-tested value, and it builds the base for larger, more complex discussions later.

Smokey and Elaine

DEFINITION: Dialogue journals are written conversations between just two people, one-to-one, like pen pals. The pair can be the teacher and a student or two students. Dialogues can be done "live," as quick exchanges during class, or as "takeaways," longer, more leisurely letters written and answered at the correspondents' convenience. Dialogue journals get every single student "talking," and thus can replace low-participation whole-class discussions. At the same time, dialogue journals keep the complexity low. It's just two people, completely accountable to each other, without the exponentially more complex dynamics of larger groups.

"Dialogue journals get every single student 'talking,' and thus can replace low-participation whole-class discussions."

VARIATIONS:

- Teacher-Student Dialogues
- Student-Student Dialogues
- Dialogue Across the Curriculum: Math, Foreign Language, Social Studies
- Feedback Loops

  o Student-Teacher Assessments

  o Behavior Support Letters

  o Student Self-Assessments

  o Kid-Kid Assessments

- Teacher Response to Student Writing
- Multi-Age Dialogue Journals

ORIGINS: You might be interested to hear that the school use of dialogue journals was pioneered by deaf educators in the 1960s and 1970s. Led by researcher Jana Staton, teachers of kids who were hearing-impaired exchanged notes with their students as a logical accommodation to the learners' communication needs. We treasure some copies of mid-1980s mimeographed newsletters from the Center for Applied Linguistics, where Staton and colleagues developed this powerful tool.

Later, the idea was picked up by regular educators, and popularized especially by Nancie Atwell in her groundbreaking 1987 work In *The Middle: Reading and Writing With Adolescents*. Atwell's students regularly exchanged "literature letters"—responses to their independent reading—with both their teacher and a student partner. All this history helps us understand why "dialogue journals" are sometimes thought of as primarily student-teacher correspondence, even though the kid-kid version is also widely used today, and featured heavily here.

QUICK LOOK:

While early in the year we use paired writing to build personal acquaintance and support, academic applications take over quickly. One classic use of dialogue journals is for partners to thoughtfully discuss *texts they are reading*—novels, stories, articles, essays, historic documents, scientific articles, math problems, or any other curriculum materials.

In Sonja Kosan's middle school class, she's introducing dialogue journals for the very first time. After explaining the process and pairing kids up, she reads aloud the grown-up picture book *The Wednesday Surprise* by Eve Bunting (which we visited with Joyce Sanchez on page 55). After hearing this sweet story of adult illiteracy, Matt and John take their first-ever shot at dialogue journals, with Mrs. K timing everyone's letter exchanges.

Photo courtesy of Comstock.

> Dear Matt,
>   How did you like the book?
> This is weird writing to you because
> I normally talk to you. I thought the
> book was cool The best part was wh
> Grandma learned how to read. If you
> had a chance would you help out
> someone who was old and and know no
> to read? Would you help someoc you
> Why or or why not What was
> your favorite part of the book?, If my
> Mom didn't know how to read
> and my daughter taught her how
> to, I would be so happy, wouldn't
> you?

> Dear John,
>   I liked the book it was very good
> I liked it when she learned to read
> also. I would help out anyone who
> didn't know how to read reading is a
> very important thing in life so is
> writing. What do you think about the
> last sentence.

> Dear Matt,
>   I never thought you

> would say or write some thing so
> touching. You just showed me
> that you are getting in touch with
> your feminine side.

While the boys are obviously suffering some first-time jitters (and Matt could use some punctuation), they've discovered a good strategy for keeping the conversation going: Throw out some good, open-ended questions, and then chew on them with your partner. That's how you get in touch with your feminine side.

Figure 4.1

Once partners have exchanged notes twice, Sonja invites them to continue the discussion of *The Wednesday Surprise* out loud for a few minutes. Finally, she convenes the whole class and asks for volunteer pairs to share one theme, thread, or topic of their conversations. Inside of 10 minutes, every student in the class has joined in a thoughtful discussion of a piece of literature—and many are eager to go public with their thinking.

LAUNCHING LESSON:

Imagine that a group of actors has come to your school this afternoon to put on a short play about the life of Abraham Lincoln. You lead your fifth graders down to the auditorium, get them seated in the correct rows, and keep an eagle eye for inattentive behavior. But the play is engaging, and the kids eat it up. Then it's off to the buses, and home for the night.

The next morning, as the kids file in, what do you do? Bubbling up from the cellular level, your teacher DNA impels you to commence a *whole-class discussion*. You instinctively ask, "So, you guys, what did you think about the play yesterday?" If you happen to be a first-grade teacher, every hand in the room will now shoot up, though most of the proffered comments turn out to be "I don't remember what I was going to say" or are unrelated to the play.

In any case, this eagerness to join in class discussions declines steeply by grade level. In most classrooms, a couple of hands go up, and other kids look blank. Thus begins the age-old school ritual in which a fraction of students speak up, and the majority sit, ignore, drift, sleep, or actively avoid participating. Since only one person can talk at once, the 29 other folks in the room can only listen the vast majority of the time. There's almost no positive social pressure on the majority of students to join in. And we wonder why kids say school is "boring."

But what if *everyone* talked about the Lincoln play? Of course, we can always put kids in groups to discuss the play, which works very nicely when kids are trained in the social skills of small-group discussion. But even then, if we split the class into a handful of groups, we still have perhaps five speakers and 25 listeners at a time. And there's no way to be sure that students actually stay on the topic.

So when the thespians rolled through her school, fifth-grade teacher Jane Cook took a different route. First she formed kids into pairs and had them pull out a blank sheet of paper and a pencil. Then she said,

> Today, we're going to talk about the play we saw yesterday, but instead of discussing it in the whole class out loud, one at a time, we're going to talk about the play with one buddy each, in writing. How can we do that? We are going to write short letters to our buddies about the play, and then pass them back and forth, like mail. Sound like fun? I'll tell you more in a minute—for now, everyone needs a partner. So come up and grab a Popsicle stick out of our partner jar and see who your buddy will be today. Sit down together and both of you get out a full-size blank sheet of paper. I'll give you a minute.
>
> OK, everybody settled? So we're going to write letters to each other about the Lincoln play—but they are going to be really short. We're only going to write for one minute, and then we are going to trade papers. What do you do when you get a letter? Right, you read it! Then what? Of course, you write back. So that's what we are going to do right now. When we pass these letters, you'll read what your pal wrote, and right underneath where they stopped, you'll write them back an answer. But this will go fast. We'll write and pass three or four times. You just keep writing, and I will keep time for you.
>
> Finally, what are you going to write about? See this list I have projected here? You may have lots of things that you remember about the play that you can't wait to talk about. If that's the case, go for it. But if you need a little reminder or a topic to give you a quick

start on your letter-writing, you can use one of these topics. I will leave them up.

- What you liked about the play

- What you thought about the people in Lincoln's family

- How you liked the acting, scenery, or costumes

- What facts you learned about Abraham Lincoln

- What questions you still have

- Anything else that comes to mind as you think back on the performance yesterday

This will be something fun and different. Everyone gets to talk—you don't have to raise your hand. And just so you know, I will be collecting these when we are done to see what you've talked about.
Ready? Let's write letters!

As kids write, Jane circulates through the room, looking over shoulders and gauging kids' progress. About every minute and a half, she instructs kids to finish the sentence they are currently working on, and then tells them to exchange papers. Then, their job is to read what their buddy has written, and respond, right under wherever their partner left off writing, keeping the conversation going. She reminds kids that they can respond, comment, connect, compare, debate a point, or shift to another play-related topic. "Just keep the conversation going," she encourages.

One pair of kids wrote this:

> March 14, 2002
> Room 104
>
> Dear, Tara
>
> How did you like the play yesterday? Do you still remember their real names? What were their names in the play? The sence was terrific.
>
> Sincerly,
>
> Anthony
> Wesley
> Warren
>
> Anthony,
> I liked the play but, I wish they showed Lincoln was shot. I don't know there real names, but the people played Abrahamn Lincoln and Mary Todd Lincoln. By the way scene is spelled S-ce-ne.
>
> signed,
> Tara ashley Snyder
>
> Dear, Tara
>
> That sounds kind of immplight that they would chow you him Aberahmn was shot. Will I did know their names. ok.
>
> Sincerly,

Figure 4.2 (continued)

Figure 4.2 (continued)

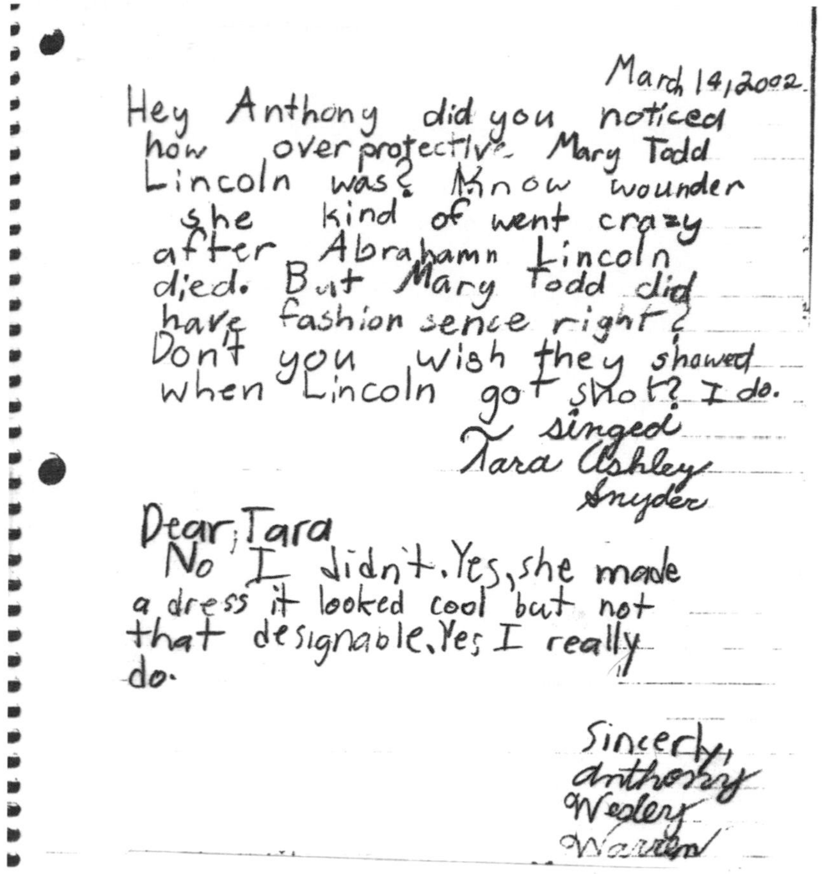

> March 14, 2002
>
> Hey Anthony did you noticed how overprotective Mary Todd Lincoln was? Know wounder she kind of went crazy after Abrahamn Lincoln died. But Mary todd did have fashion sence right? Don't you wish they showed when Lincoln got shot? I do.
>
> singed
> Tara Ashley Snyder
>
> Dear; Tara
> No I didn't. Yes, she made a dress it looked cool but not that designable. Yes I really do.
>
> Sincerly,
> anthony Wesley Warren

a Mary Todd Lincoln was shown sewing during the play.

b Here you might think that Anthony has gone completely off the rails, until you look up and notice that he is answering Tara's questions one by one. We suspect that his final agreement that, yes, the play should have included Lincoln's fatal shooting may not be wholehearted.

Figure 4.2

Most importantly, if you had walked into the room while kids were writing these notes back and forth, you would have been struck by the fact *that every single kid in the room* was either writing or reading about the play for about eight solid minutes. Every kid—no sleepers, no slackers.

This reminds us: If you want engagement, you can have it. You just have to use the classroom structures that trigger active learning instead of stifling it, as lectures can. Written conversations make it easy for everyone, bold or shy, to participate.

GENERAL INSTRUCTIONS FOR "LIVE" DIALOGUE JOURNALS

Below are the instructions as we tell them to kids:

- Sit next to your chosen or assigned partner. Get in a good position for both writing and talking, and be sure you can still see any materials I project on the screen. *This might include the instructions for this activity, a list of possible letter-starter phrases, or text or an image that is the subject of the writing.*

- Everyone please get a full-size blank piece of paper ready to use. Put your name in the upper left-hand margin. Then, just below your name, write a "salutation" to your partner, as in "Dear . . ." Now you are ready to have a dialogue journal with your pal.

- As we write letters, please follow these rules:

1. Use your best handwriting so your partner can understand you.

2. Don't worry about spelling and grammar. Just get your thoughts out.

3. Draw pictures, diagrams, or cartoons if that helps you make your point.

4. Use all the time I give you for writing. Keep that pen moving until I tell you to exchange papers.

5. No talking. This is a silent activity.

- Papers ready? OK. You are all going to write your buddy a letter on our topic, and then "mail it" by exchanging notes. You are both going to be writing letters at the same time. You're not waiting or watching your partner—you're both writing all the time. It'll make sense in a minute!
The writing time will be pretty short, just about one or two minutes per letter. I'll give you a warning when there are 15 seconds left each time.

- Go ahead and write your partner about your thoughts, reactions, questions, or feelings about our topic. *The topic can be any common experience: a story, poem, nonfiction article, lab experiment, or textbook selection. If you want to be sure that all kids can get started writing promptly, you may decide to project four or five possible "safety net" starter stems (e.g., "One thing I am wondering is . . ."), but remove these after the first note-passing so kids can then focus on responding to their partner's ideas. For a list of useful writing prompts, both general and subject specific, see pages 66–69.*

Keep time not by exact minutes and seconds, but by walking and watching kids write. When most students have filled a quarter of a page, it is time to pass.

- OK, time to "mail your letters." Exchange with your partner. Now read your buddy's note, and think about it a little bit. Then, just beneath their letter, write back for . . . minutes. You can tell your reaction, make a comment, ask questions, share a connection you've made, agree or disagree, or raise a whole new idea. Just keep the conversation going! *Walk the room, looking over shoulders to get the timing right.*

- Pass again, please. Repeat and continue. *Usually three or four notes is just right. Don't time this activity by actual minutes, but by watching how kids are coming and by calling "Pass" only when most people have written at least a few lines.*

OPTIONAL SHARING OUT: Sometimes, these pair conversations, just like out-loud turn-and-talks, have inherent value and needn't be shared or debriefed (and we can always collect them, of course). But other times, we want to use the thinking from dialogue journals to advance the curricular work at hand.

- Let's gather as a whole class and see what new learning or questions came out of this dialogue journaling. Will a few pairs please share one highlight, one thread of your discussion? Something you spent time on, something that sparked lively discussion, maybe something you argued or laughed or wondered about? *And now you can connect kids' comments to the subject under study.*

ADJUSTMENTS FOR "TAKEAWAY" DIALOGUE JOURNALS

- Live dialogue journals, as described above, are usually done by the whole class at once, with the teacher doing the timing, and the letters being written, received, and answered immediately. Kind of like texting. Takeaway dialogue journals are more leisurely, and operate more like regular letters or emails.

- Kids write their partner a note when their schedule permits (sometimes as homework), taking whatever time they need to offer a thoughtful missive. Typically, these notes are longer and more carefully composed than speedy live dialogue journals. They are "mailed" by simple hand delivery, via email, or by placing them in the partner's classroom mailbox—a system that teachers who use this strategy often set up.

- Recipients answer dialogue journals when they have time to think about and thoughtfully respond to their partner's notes. They return them through the same channel they arrived.

- These "takeaway" dialogue journals sometimes go on for weeks or longer. Many teachers start these more sustained conversations a bit later in the year, allowing students to request their own long-term partners.

© Getty Images.

TEACHER-STUDENT DIALOGUES

Purpose: When teachers correspond with individual students, they can offer a carefully targeted personal "conference" that guides learning.

Literacy instruction changed forever in American schools when the "workshop" model came into wide use. At the core of workshop is the one-to-one conference, where the teacher regularly sits down to coach each young reader and writer, face-to-face, for a few minutes. These quick individual meetings are so valuable that we move heaven and earth to make them possible. A commitment to conferring requires highly efficient classroom management and training; if you are having a private conference with one kid, what are the other 29 class members doing?

For primary-age kids, one of the most valuable written dialogues we can initiate is when we sit down beside one child, with a blank sheet of paper and one pen in front of us. Here, Sarah's teacher initiates a written conversation by writing a question—and vocalizing it as the words go down on the page—"What did you do this weekend?" Then she hands Sarah the pen and invites her to respond. They go back and forth for a while, sharing one pen.

> **a** →
> What did you do this week-end? MZM
>
> WOT DDUDO ?
>
> I went on a canoe Trip I went to Lake Michigan.

a → Sarah says "Museum. What did you do?"

Figure 4.3

There's a lot going on in this special dialogue: The teacher is modeling adult text, and Sarah is watching it go down on the page. Both parties are fully engaged since the topic is mutually agreed upon. The trick is to find time to do this with every student in a classroom! But this kind of written dialogue can easily be taught to aides, parents, and older kids, so it doesn't always have to be the teacher doing the one-on-one.

Nancie Atwell showed many of us how written dialogues can potentiate great book talks between teachers and individual students. Though her examples came from the middle grades, the idea comfortably stretches down to kindergarten and up through high school. Here, Susan Smith's third graders have just read a short article about Martin Luther King. Now she asks kids to write her a note in response. Here's what Pam shared.

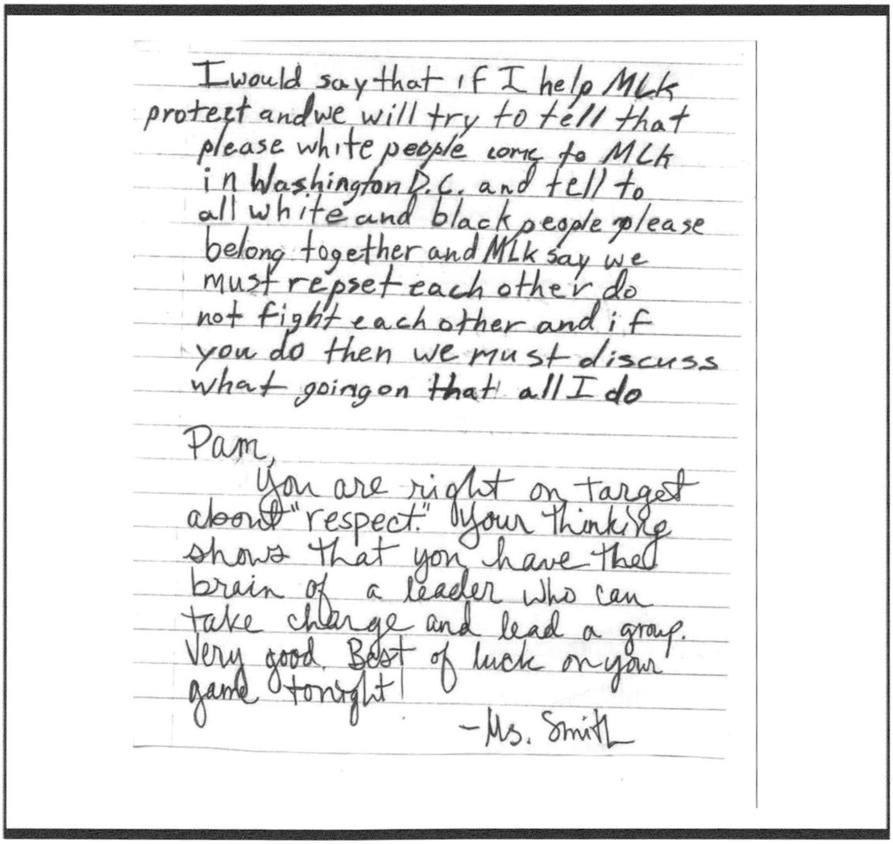

I would say that if I help MLk protest and we will try to tell that please white people come to MLk in Washington D.C. and tell to all white and black people please belong together and MLk say we must repset each other do not fight each other and if you do then we must discuss what going on that all I do

Pam,
You are right on target about "respect." Your thinking shows that you have the brain of a leader who can take charge and lead a group. Very good. Best of luck on your game tonight!
—Ms. Smith

Figure 4.4

Notice how Susan not only gives Pam some supportive feedback on the curricular topic, but also shows personal interest by wishing Pam well in her upcoming game. We are never done building friendliness and support in our classrooms.

In her special education class, Kelly Beauchamp uses dialogue journals to support her kids' reading. After reading aloud *Verdi* by Janell Cannon, Kelly had this written conversation with Andrea about the story—and about journaling itself.

Dear Mrs. Beauchamp,

I love this story becase it is like a life cycle and life cycle is where it goes like a generation.

Andrea

Dear Andrea,

That is so true and I am so proud of you for making that connection. Kind of like I am in another generation than you, but I still like to dance and have fun.

Mrs B

Dear Mrs. Beauchamp,

Verdi was a very good story to read and conect to and maybe this will help me reading better cause it helps on reading, writing, and thinking.

Andrea

Dear Andrea,

You are going to make me cry! I am so proud of you for realizing that this lesson can help us all be better readers, writers, and thinkers.

Mrs. B

Dear Mrs. Beauchamp,

I loved it and I think we need to do this on everything we read. The story I loved it and it also means never give up—in case your age but if you want to change it is your decision not theirs! And I think you're doing a good job! You are the greatest teacher in the world! You are pretty or cute in your own way.

Andrea

As with Kelly and Andrea, teacher-student dialogues can be quick, one-time events. Or, they can become the very fiber of classroom life all year long. Seventh-grade teacher Jill Vander Viren maintains regular "takeaway" dialogue journals among herself and her young readers.

Dear Miss Vander Viren,

I'm reading *Across Five Aprils* now. I'm on about page 50. From what I've read so far it's kind of hard to imagine what's happening. It's kind of slow. Does it get any better? Are there any other books by Irene Hunt that you know of?

Sincerely,

Susan

Dear Susan,

I know, *Across Five Aprils* is difficult to understand/get into, but in the end I think you'll like the story. You'll get to know Shad, Jeremy and the narrator very well (plus you'll learn more about the Civil War).

Other books by Hunt include *Up a Road Slowly* (it sounds good) and *William*. *Across Five Aprils* is taken from stories her grandfather told her about the Civil War!

Ms. V

Teachers sometimes worry about saying "the right thing" when they respond to student letters. But, as Jill's answer shows, the real job is just to be authentic and relevant. Here, Jill simply offers some support and background info to a student who's struggling to get into a novel.

Figure 4.5

While Jill writes weekly notes to each student, every kid is also matched up with a student partner, and they exchange literature letters on the same schedule. Greg and Doug are staying in touch with each other, and with Ms. Vander Viren, as they work their way through some books.

NN 2

Letter #9B

Dear Greg,   ~9-10~

Hi! Im about half way through *Call of the Wild* now and its real good. The whole story is told from a dog's point of view, and so far there's been a lot of blood and guts. It has a lot to do with honor and courage, even if the subject is only a dog. The book was written in 1903 and has been popular for 86 years! What are you reading?

Figure 4.6

I'm half way through *The Dark Secret of Weatherend*, by John Bellairs. Its About this insane guy who is using magic to wipe out the world, It's pretty weird, but good.

Greg

Figure 4.7

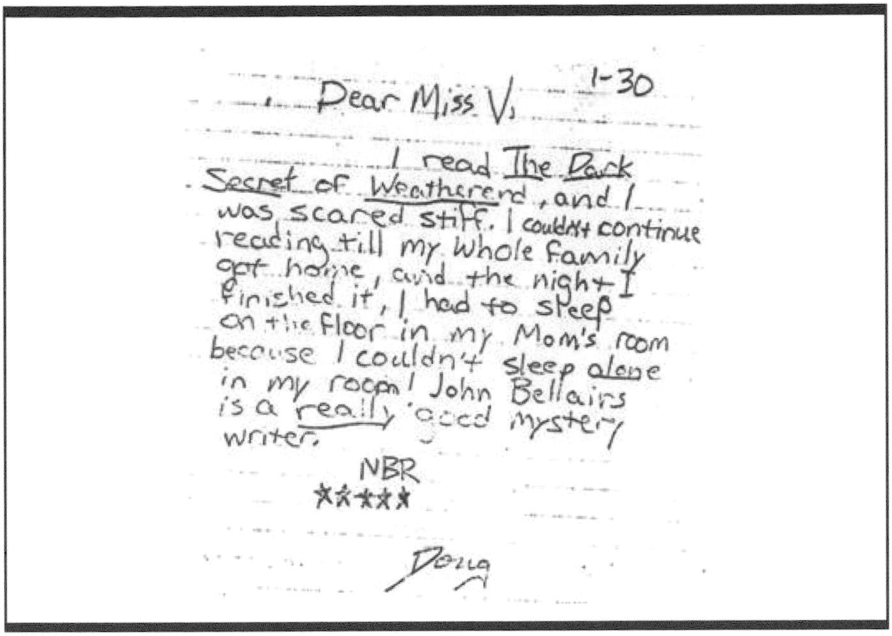

> Dear Miss V, 1-30
>
> I read *The Dark Secret of Weatherend*, and I was scared stiff. I couldn't continue reading till my whole family got home, and the night I finished it, I had to sleep on the floor in my Mom's room because I couldn't sleep alone in my room! John Bellairs is a really good mystery writer.
>
> NBR
> ★★★★★
>
> Doug

Jill's kids enjoy making up their own book-rating star systems, just like the grown-up critics. Here Doug Nelson has created the NBR (Nelson Book Rating) guide.

Figure 4.8

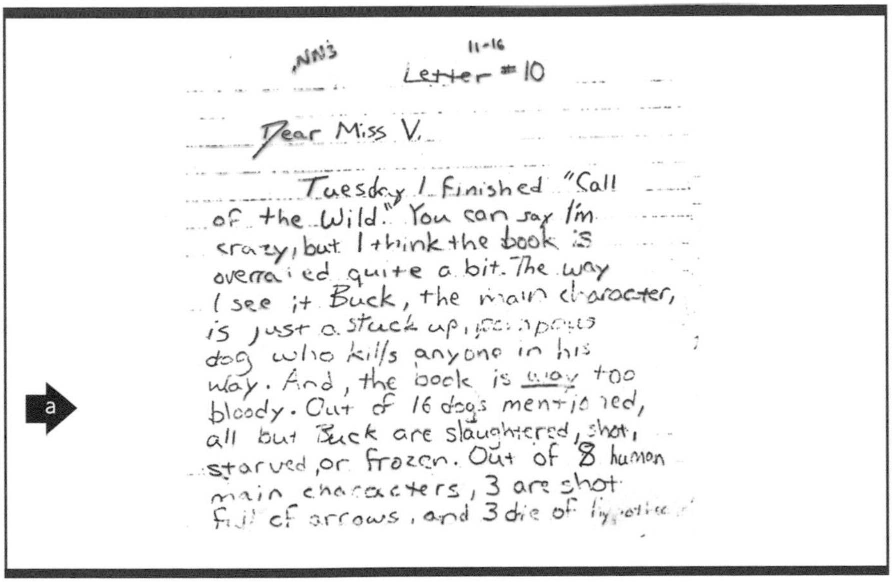

> NN3   11-16
>   Letter #10
>
> Dear Miss V,
>
> Tuesday I finished "Call of the Wild." You can say I'm crazy, but I think the book is overrated quite a bit. The way I see it Buck, the main character, is just a stuck up, pompous dog who kills anyone in his way. And, the book is way too bloody. Out of 16 dogs mentioned, all but Buck are slaughtered, shot, starved, or frozen. Out of 8 human main characters, 3 are shot full of arrows, and 3 die of hypothermia

Talk about textual evidence! Doug really delivers the proof that Jack London's classic is über-violent. And then he only gives it one and a half stars. Snap!

Figure 4.9 (continued)

N.B.R.
Call of The Wild ⭐$!

Sincerely, Doug

PS

It appears I did avg. 20 pages.
(or just about)

$$9\overline{)172}$$

b Here, Doug is calculating his pages-per-day reading rate.

Figure 4.9

Mary Ellen and Erin were already enthusiastic readers, and their letters developed into a fierce but fictional book-reviewer rivalry. At one point Erin suggested that they go into the library, cover their eyes, and pick a book to read at random. Having accepted this arbitrary challenge, Mary Ellen fired off the mock-outraged riposte on the facing page:

Photo courtesy of Creatas.

Dear Erin,

Boy would I like to hit you 1 ! Never again will I ever pick a book off the shelves with my eyes closed! But, for my honor's sake I read, painfully, The House of Seven Gables. It took me 3 long, boring, sick days to read this long, boring book. I will never again even to hear this title's name without getting sick. This book is definitely not for our age group + not on my top list. I give Nathanial Hawthorne's House of Seven Gables a ☆ . (half one star).

Mary "Ellen"

P.S. - read in peace. (well maybe not you!!)
P.P.S. - this was pure torture!!!
#3

Notice that Mary Ellen actually read *The House of Seven Gables* in just three days! And hated it. But for a reader as voracious as she is, that's simply too long to spend on any one book.

Figure 4.10

Dear Mary Ellen,

You must broaden your horizons! The House of Seven Gables will enrich you, and someday you will thank me for making you read it!

Read in Peace!

Love,
Erin

P.S. I own all rights to the phrase "Read in Peace!" It is copyrighted under patent number 2,654,953,711. Any copying, duplication, or reproducing of said phrase is prohibited and offenders will be prosecuted by law. Any time it is written, it can and will be used against you in a court of law! Good day!

a Bring on the lawyers!

Figure 4.11

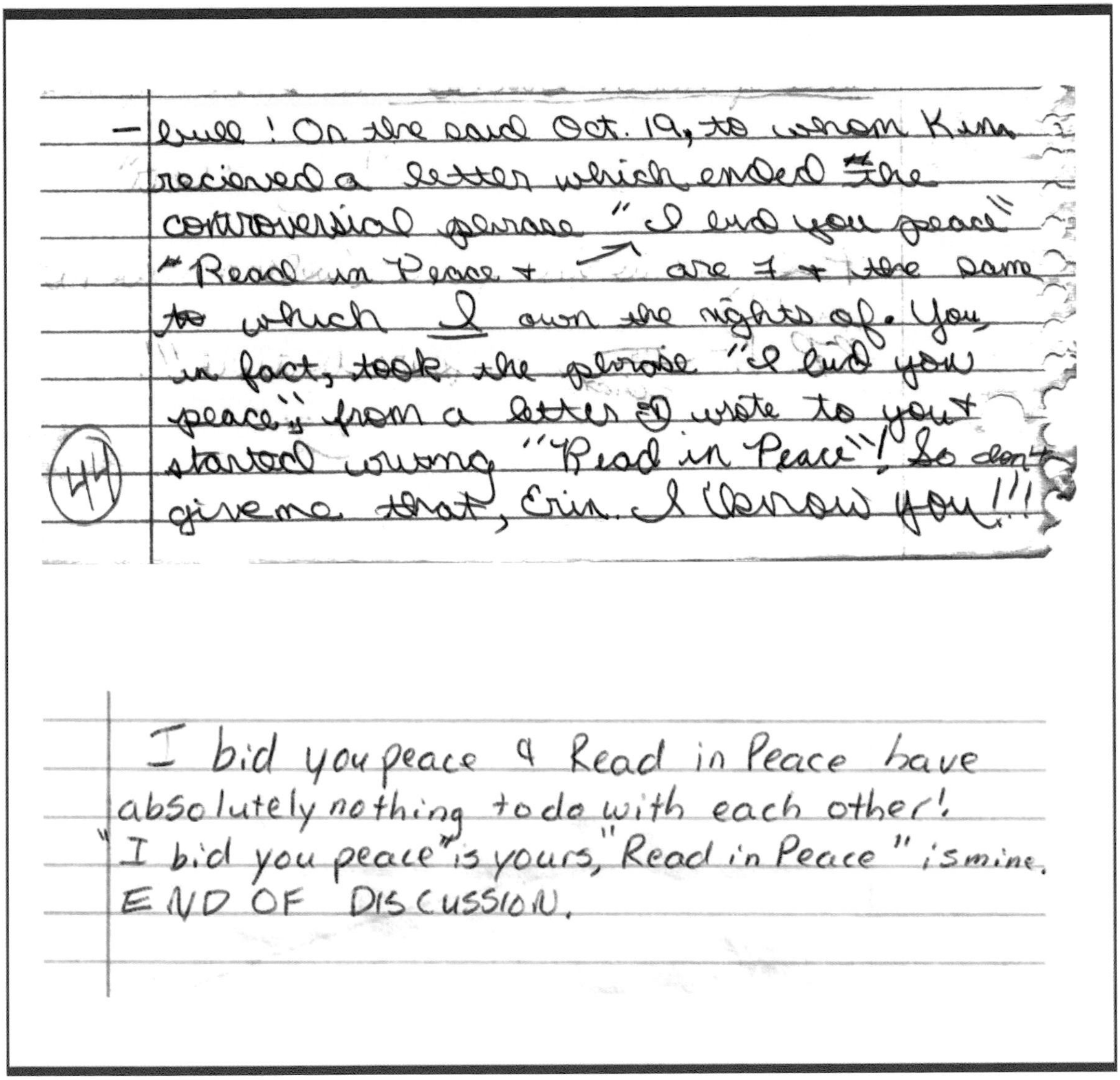

— Well! On the said Oct. 19, to whom Kim recieved a letter which ended the controversial phrase "I end you peace" "Read in Peace" and → are ≠ the same to which I own the rights of. You, in fact, took the phrase "I end you peace" from a letter I wrote to you + started wrong "Read in Peace"! So don't give me that, Erin. I know you!!!

(44)

I bid you peace & Read in Peace have absolutely nothing to do with each other! "I bid you peace" is yours, "Read in Peace" is mine. END OF DISCUSSION.

Figure 4.12

Jill was convulsed over this exchange.

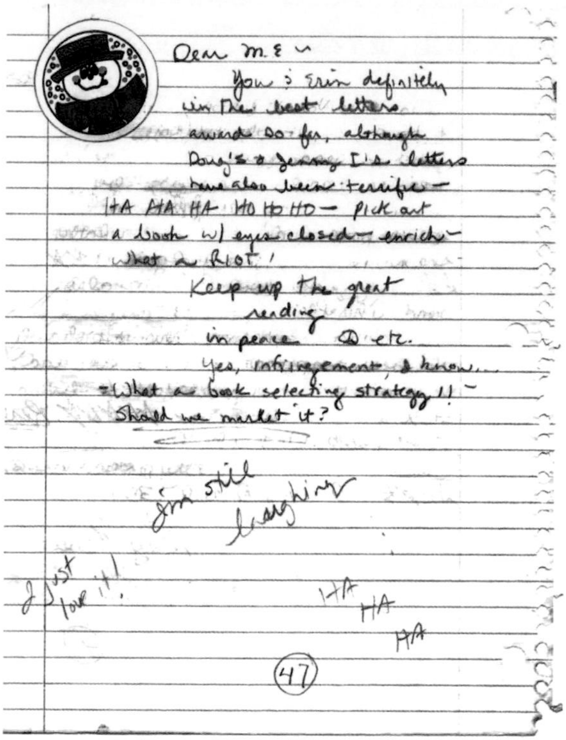

Dear Mary Ellen,

You and Erin definitely win the prize for most unusual letters so far:

HA HA HA HO HO HO—pick out a book with eyes closed—"enrich"—What a RIOT!

Keep up the great Reading in Peace etc. (Yes, I've infringed on your copyright, I know . . .) What a book selecting strategy! Should we market it?

I'm still laughing. I just love it!

HA HA HA

Ms V

Figure 4.13

STUDENT-STUDENT DIALOGUES

Purpose: When pairs of students engage in "live" written conversations during class, everyone has a chance to engage, think, react, respond, and question the subject matter.

The big payoff with dialogue journals comes when kids are writing to each other, not just to us. A natural time for dialogue journals is while students are reading a whole novel or nonfiction book.

Our colleague Erin Ripple at Federal Hocking High School asked her freshmen to have a written conversation about the opening pages of *The Hunger Games*.

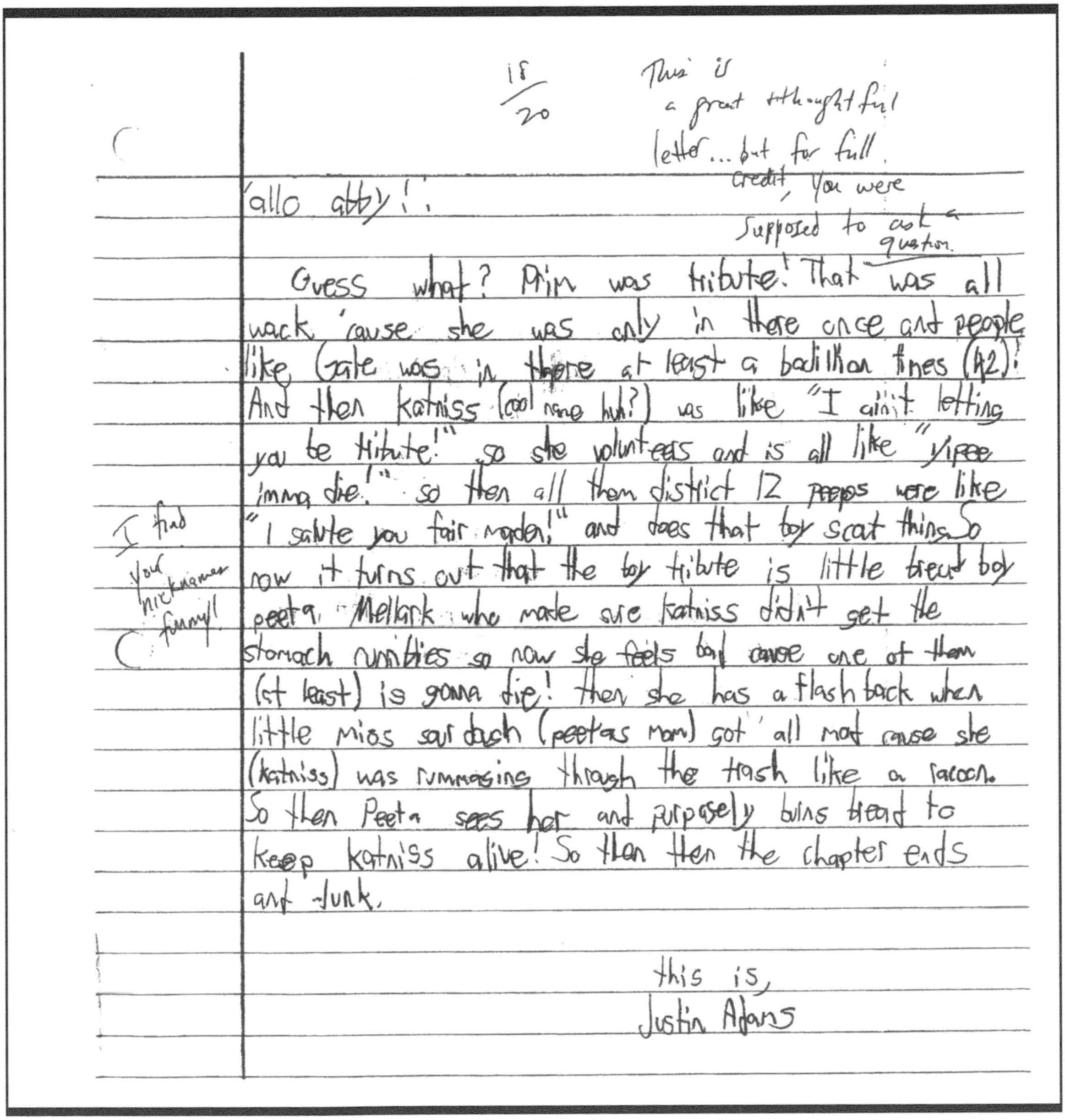

> 18/20
>
> This is a great thoughtful letter... but for full credit, you were supposed to ask a question.
>
> 'allo abby!,
>
> Guess what? Prim was tribute! That was all wack 'cause she was only in there once and people like Gale was in there at least a bajillion times (h2). And then Katniss (cool name huh?) was like "I ain't letting you be tribute!" so she volunteers and is all like "yipee imma die." so then all them district 12 peeps were like "I salute you fair maden!" and does that boy scat thing. So now it turns out that the boy tribute is little bread boy peeta Mellark who made sure katniss didn't get the stomach rumblies so now she feels bad 'cause one of them (at least) is gonna die! then she has a flashback when little miss sour dough (peeta's mom) got all mad 'cause she (katniss) was rummaging through the trash like a racoon. So then Peeta sees her and purposely burns bread to keep katniss alive! So then then the chapter ends and junk.
>
> *(margin note:)* I find your nicknames funny!
>
> this is,
> Justin Adams

In addition to being a clever character piece, Justin's letter also offers a solid plot summary of the first few chapters.

Figure 4.14

Dear Justin,

I thought District 12's reaction to Katniss volunteering was really great and really special. Apparently, that reaction doesn't happen too often.

Peeta was totally amazing for giving Katniss the bread, especially because he probably knew his mom would get mad.

I thought Peeta's mom was really mean and that her anger was kind of too much and unnecessary. I mean, I get that she would be mad, but THAT mad? Katniss was a starving 11-year-old for Christ's sake!

I guess that's about it.

Sincerely,
Abby Conrad

P.S.
Your letter totally cracked me up

a   More good textual evidence and a critical character appraisal.

Figure 4.15

Justin's letter is truly a tour de force of faux gangsterese. If you find something funnier, please send it to us immediately. Meanwhile, Erin still has her game face on, enforcing the requirement that you have to pose at least one question for full credit.

TWO MEANS TWO

We have both done this a thousand times: Tell students to "grab a partner," and then plunge into some pair activity without making sure that kids are really two by two. Have you done this? And seen some kids pick one partner, some pick two, some pick none, and some pick five? Obviously if we fail to police this, we get asymmetrical groups that will be having totally different experiences as the activity unfolds. The solo kids will have no one to talk to, the kids in oversized groups won't get enough airtime or accountability, and so forth.

So we have to be tough—and do the math. When you put a class of kids in pairs there are only two possible outcomes. Either everyone has one partner, or there is just one singleton left over. That person can become the teacher's partner or a member of the only group of three that's allowed to form.

Elaine: In my class this year we've been doing a lot of reading about identity and sense of self, both personally and culturally. It occurred to me that investigating the word and concept "macho" with my New Mexican students might be a worthwhile endeavor. In this two-stage process, I first asked them what they thought the word *macho* meant to them. In this conversation between Ria and Cody are echoes from a previous discussion on what "abuse" means.

Ria: Macho: A Man who thinks he is powerful/strong mentally and physically. A man who thinks he has the upper hand in anything or anyone.

Cody: I think your description of macho is a good one. I agree because a macho man would want everything done his way. They want

Preconceived notions of what "macho" means surfaced here. A word prevalent in American culture comes into focus in this conversation.

control of everyone around them. If someone has control, then the macho man sees that as a threat. I think you are a very strong woman for leaving a situation like that. I can't even begin to imagine what you went through, but you got through it. And I'm happy you have. I love you!

Ria: I'm not sorry I told you.

After this "flip-flop" conversation, I gave them an excerpt from an article "'I'm the King': The Macho Image" by Rudolfo Anaya, one of our finest local and national writers. The article focuses on the word *macho* itself and the historical meanings of the word and concept. A key passage reads

> Drunkenness, abusing women, raising hell (all elements of la vida loca) are some mistaken conceptions of what macho means . . . young men acting contrary to the good of their community have not yet learned the real essence of maleness.

Here's how some students responded to Anaya's thoughts, and to each other:

Dear Girardo,

It has changed my opinion because what Rudolfo Anaya said about macho being a learned behavior and it being misunderstood as any aspect of hispanic/Latino culture. It is a mistaken concept of drunkenness, abusing women, and raising hell. It is a negative behavior aped by a new generation.

Dear John,

To me I still think macho is someone who acts tough because it's all I've seen it as. I've never been told or showed macho can be a good thing till now after having read this article. It's going to take some time for me to switch my views about Macho. To me macho ain't much. To act Puro ("real") is better. Act yourself and you got nothing to prove.

Dear Girardo,

I saw macho as a more negative word for me. But your list and the article gave me a different look on the word. I would have to say that my great grandfather was one of the most macho men I ever knew. He was very respectful, honest, open-hearted, hard-working and always provided for my grandmother and the kids no matter what.

Here Girardo and John delve further into their concepts of "macho" after reading the Anaya article.

In their conversations, my mostly Hispanic and Native students really resonated with this issue. And many of them seemed to be thinking hard about Anaya's assertion that "young men acting contrary to the good of their community have not yet learned the real essence of maleness."

DIALOGUE JOURNALS ACROSS THE CURRICULUM

Purpose: When students are studying math, science, social studies, or any other school subject, paired written conversations allow everyone to join in the thinking.

Math

We most frequently see dialogue journals being used in language arts or English classes, and that's a missed opportunity. The structure is an equally powerful way to get kids thinking in any content area. At Federal Hocking High School in Stewart, Ohio, teacher Sue Collins routinely uses written conversation to help students practice mathematical thinking. Here's one assignment she presented:

Solve the following equation, show all the steps, and check your solution.

$$-2x + 7 = 11$$

Solve the following inequality, show all the steps, and check your solution.

$$-2x + 7 \leq 11$$

When you have finished solving and checking your solutions, have a dialogue journal with your partner, comparing and contrasting the processes and the solutions to the equation and the inequality.

Here are some of the dialogues kids wrote during the last step of the assignment:

Pair 1

I noticed that these two problems were similar because most of both of the problems followed the same rules.

I noticed that too, but the inequality had some extra rules.

Yeah you know you have a good point.

I noticed the difference in these problems was that for the second one the check is a little bit harder 'cause unlike #1 you have to check by using two #s.

Yeah, but it was still easy for me to remember the rules of it.

Well, it's harder for me because I am a tad bit slower in learning, but I get your drift.

Pair 2

The equation and inequality involved all the same numbers. You ended up subtracting 7 from 11 on both problems. But the equation you have only one answer and the inequality you have a lot of answers. The 1st check was easier. ☺

I like this part. . . . I never thought of that . . . other than that we wrote the same thing.

Yeah, I didn't think about the checks being different. But other than that we wrote the exactly same stuff. Smarty pants!

Yep, I'm hungry. There is nothing else to write.

Pair 3

The difference between two inequalities were that in the first one only one answer could be right and the second one any number greater than −2 was right.

The first problem was an equation, not an inequality!

Oh so what! You know what I meant!

No, actually I was like "what is she talking about?" Get it right Lauren! They are different. You get an answer with an equation and a bunch of possible answers with an inequality. You use a graph with an inequality like this.

You're a jerk!

Am not! Just smart.

Once again, we'd point out the mixture of good thinking, reflection, and playfulness in these notes. The kids are on-topic for sure—but the personal connection, banter, and humor help sustain energy for the work.

Foreign Language

For many years, smart foreign language teachers have been inviting pairs of students to practice the target language in short partner conversations like these. The rule is to write in the new language the best you can; when you come to a vocab item you don't know, just plug in the English word and carry on.

Hola Derek, porque tú el fútbol americano equipo es muy malo?

~~Porque Steve Miceli.~~

Porque Steve Miceli es muy mal, et no inteligente.

Por que ~~tienes un bloom~~ tu estas el músculos pequeño?

~~Mi~~ Mi músculos es dos talla tú músculos. ¿Tú quieres la lucha libre varsity?

Si, quiero la lucha libre varsity, et tú, tú quieres la lucha libre varsity en lunes contra Grays Lake et Lake Zurich?

Si, yo ~~soy~~ voy la lucha libre varsity! ~~es~~ La lucha libre practicar es muy ~~cansado~~. ~~deses~~ cansado, no.

Si, qué pena Mahron tengo un problema de la pierna

¡Adios Derek!
Adios A.J. ~~tienes va~~ yo voy a practicar hoy

Los muchachos se divierten en practicando español!   Figure 4.16

Often foreign language teachers have kids doing these conversations right at the start of class, as a warm-up to the target language.

Social Studies

Sara Ahmed's seventh-grade history class is studying freedom of speech and censorship. For a contemporary example, Sara has brought in articles about a recent contoversy in Arizona. For many years, high schools in Tuscon offered a special course about Hispanic and Chicano history in the Southwest. Among other outcomes, graduates of this class scored higher on college entrance exams than did other students in the school. But while nonminority students could and did enroll in this course, some politicians came to see it as subversive and racially polarizing. A battle ensued, which ended with the course being abolished and its texts removed from the schools. Not exactly a book burning, but pretty close.

Sara invited Louis Urrea, one of the designers of the course, to visit her classroom and tell his side of the story. After his presentation, Sara suggested that kids jot down their reactions indvidually. Though she's a big user of dialogues, Sara hadn't set this writing up with partners. No matter, Athee and Loren got into it on their own (see Figure 4.17).

The gestalt? A pretty lively conversation, with arrows, rejoinders, bullet points— and a school of fish swimming through the middle! Not so easy to read, though. Here's a transcription of how the writing went down, as best Athee and Loren could reconstruct the sequence.

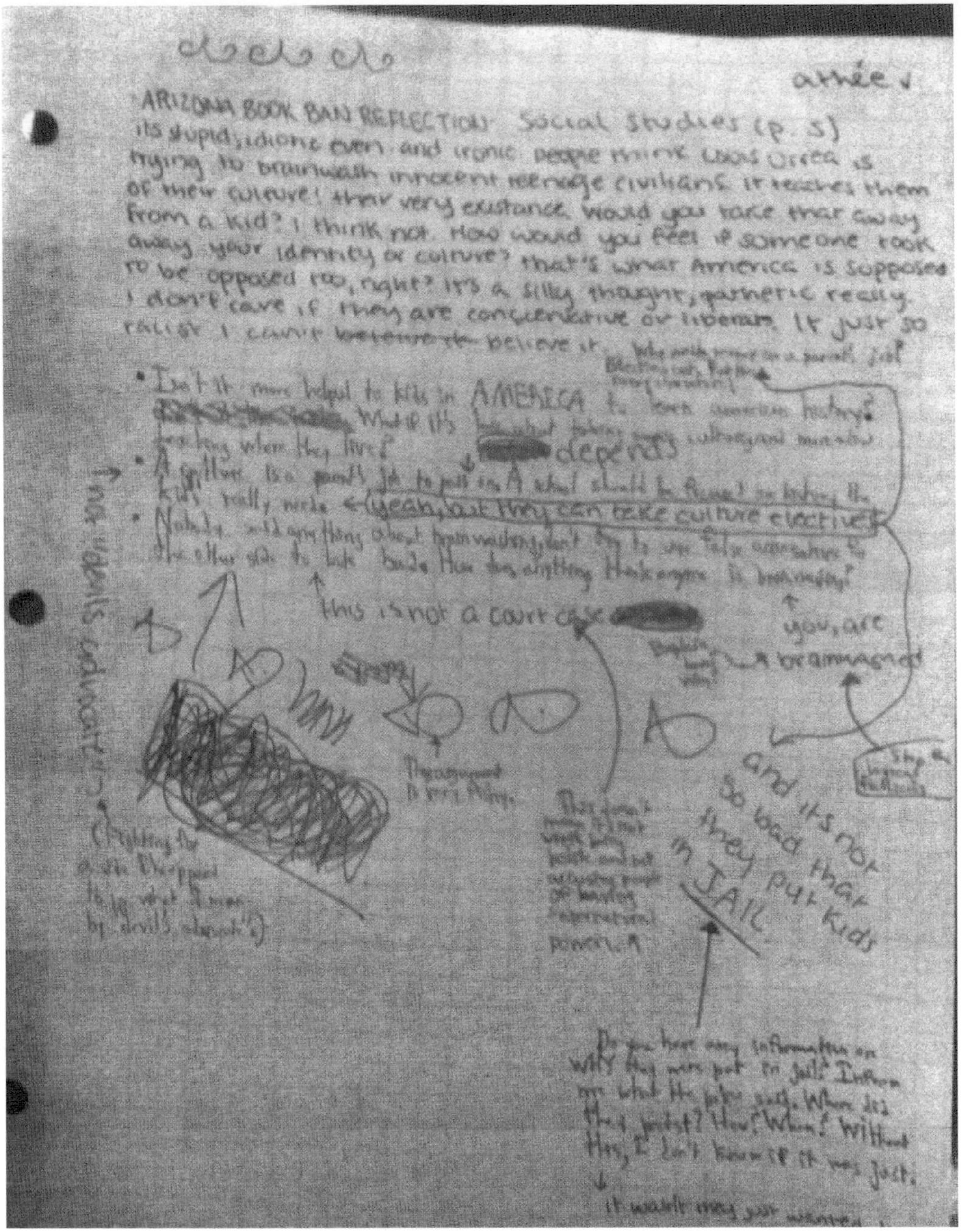

athée ✓

ARIZONA BOOK BAN REFLECTION Social Studies (p. 5)

its stupid, idiotic even and ironic people think [illegible] is trying to brainwash innocent teenage civilians. it teaches them of their culture! their very existance. would you take that away from a kid? I think not. How would you feel if someone took away your identity or culture? that's what America is supposed to be opposed too, right? it's a silly thought, pathetic really. I don't care if they are conservative or liberals. It just so [illegible] I can't ~~[illegible]~~ believe it.

depends

yeah, but they can take culture electives

this is not a court case

you, are brainwashed

and it's not so bad that they put kids in JAIL

Do you have any information on why they were put in jail? Inform me what the judge said. When did they protest? How? When? Without this, I don't know if it was just.

Figure 4.17

a Something is fishy here.

Athee

Student B

ARIZONA BOOK BAN REFLECTION
Social Studies (p. 5)

It is stupid, idiotic, and ironic that people think Louis Urrea is trying to brainwash innocent teenage civilians. It teaches them of their culture! Their very existence. Would you take that away from a kid? I think not. How would you feel if someone took away your identity or culture? That's what America is supposed to be opposed to, right? It's a silly thought, pathetic really. I don't care if they are conservatives or liberals. It's just so racist I can't believe it.

Isn't it more helpful for kids in AMERICA to learn American history? What if it's less about taking away culture and more about teaching where they live?

A culture is a parent's job to pass on. The "devils advocate." *Fighting for a side that I'm opposed to is what I mean by devil's advocate."* Depends. *A school should be focused on the history kids really need.* Yeah but they can take culture electives.

Why waste money on a parent's job? Electives cost. Put this money elsewhere!

Nobody said anything about brainwashing, don't try to use false accusations for the other side to look bad. This is not a court case. *This does not mean that it's not worth being polite and not accusing people of having supernatural powers.*

How does anything think anyone is "brainwashing?" You are brainwashed! *Explain. How? Why? Stop the logical fallacies!*

This argument is very fishy (draws a string of fish across the page).

And it's not so bad that they put kids in <u>JAIL.</u>

Do you have any information on WHY they were not put in jail? Inform me what the police said. Where did they protest? How? When? Without this I don't know if it was just.

It wasn't, they just wanted their classes. The man who boxed these books hasn't been to <u>1</u> class to see.

Looking back on their discussion, the kids sent this email for us teacher-readers to consider.

Hey Smokey,

Ms. Ahmed said you'd be using our written conversation about Arizona's book bannings to publish in a book. We'd be honored if you want to use it, neither of us expected this activity to be considered brilliant.

Sorry about the messy handwriting and the fish—we would have been a bit neater if we expected it to be published. :)

This started with Ms. Ahmed telling us to do a response journal entry about the book banning in Arizona and Luis Urrea, but we guess it turned out to be a debate on whether or not ethnic studies are a good thing for students in America. (Even though both of us thought they were good, I figured it would be fun to fight for the other side—thus turning to be the "devil's advocate".)

This is awkward.

> —Athee (it's like a-tay, and I'm a girl) and Loren (lo-ren, Male). :)

PS: The fish were an accident.

Yay! Thank you!

Figure 4.18

No, thank *you*, Athee and Loren.

FEEDBACK LOOPS

Purpose: Everyone in the classroom has reasons to give responses and feedback to others; written conversations make that process quiet, thoughtful, and private.

Student-Teacher Assessments

We teachers are accustomed to giving students feedback about their work, but we often forget (for some mysterious reason!) to ask them for their feedback on *us*. If we do want to hear from kids through a safe, private channel, a dialogue journal is the just-right vehicle. And most of the time, kids' responses will make us feel good.

Subj: Math Journal, October 24
Date: 10/24/13
From: vivian236
To: mperkins

Dear Mr. Perkins,

Last year I hated mental math or problem solving, but this year I love your "stumpers" because I've finally learned how to do them. Several times I've gotten the right answer to the daily stumper and I felt great satisfaction. It just makes me feel good, and sometimes even though I have an incorrect answer, I still feel delighted because I tried! Now I know that I hated problem-solving so much last year simply because I didn't know how to think logically. But now my mind has learned how to think carefully, step by step, using only the information that is necessary. And then, after I have figured out the answer, I look at it and ask myself one more question: Does the answer make sense? This is just one easy, simple method to guide you when solving a problem. I'm just so anxious and can't wait to learn more this year!

Vivian V.

---

a This ingratiating note also shows Vivian's understanding of an important mathematical principle—checking for reasonableness.

Figure 4.19

Wouldn't you love to have Vivian in *your* class this year?

After teaching an extended inquiry circles unit, Smokey asked his Santa Fe sixth graders to share their reactions to the process, and here's what Devin had to say.

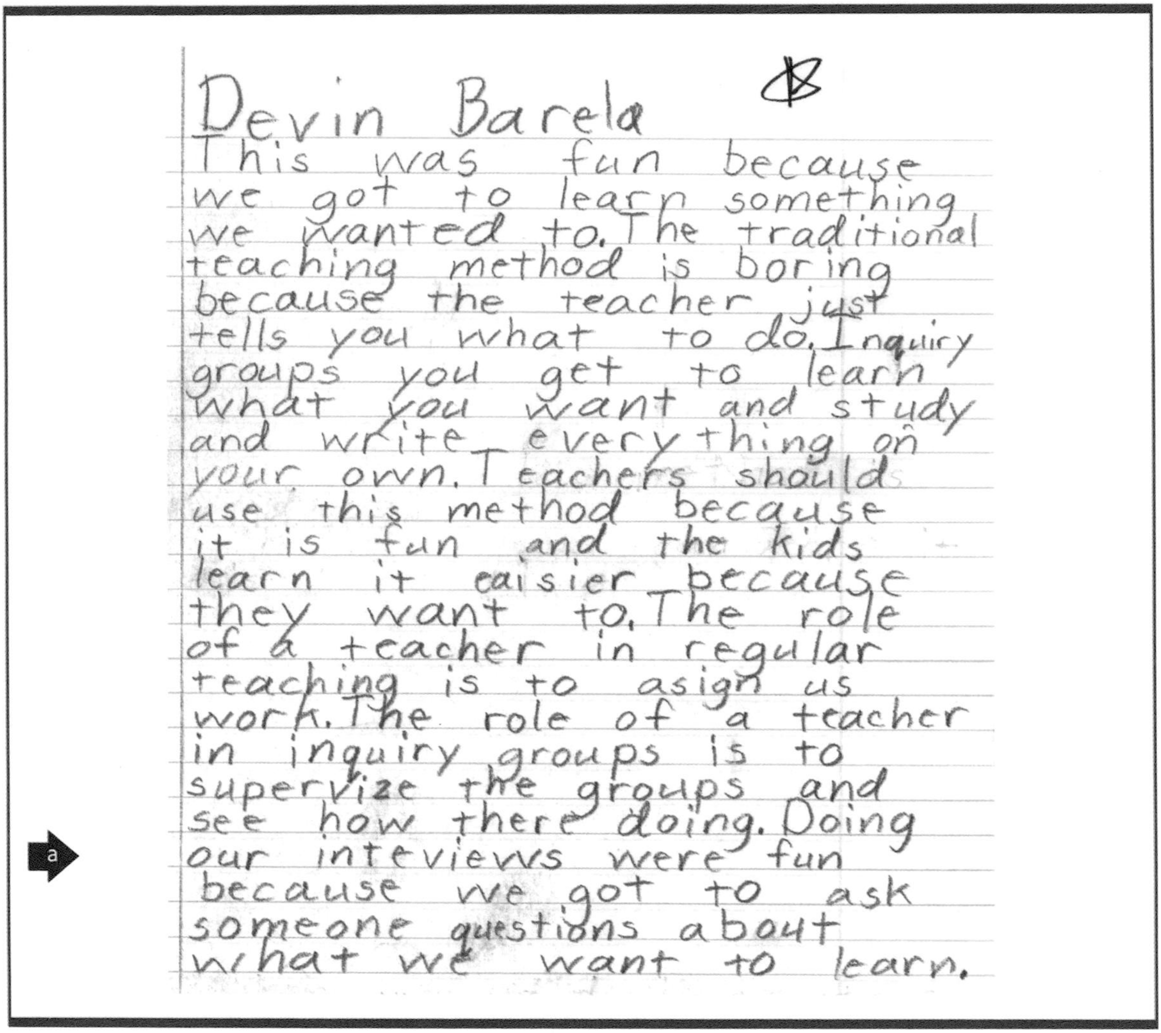

Devin Barela

This was fun because we got to learn something we wanted to. The traditional teaching method is boring because the teacher just tells you what to do. Inquiry groups you get to learn what you want and study and write everything on your own. Teachers should use this method because it is fun and the kids learn it eaisier because they want to. The role of a teacher in regular teaching is to asign us work. The role of a teacher in inquiry groups is to supervize the groups and see how there doing. Doing our inteviews were fun because we got to ask someone questions about what we want to learn.

a   In this particular inquiry circle project, each group was required to do a phone interview with at least one expert in the field of their research topic.

Figure 4.20

Whew, that's a nice validation of this particular unit, but a pretty sweeping critique of school business as usual, from the kids'-eye view.

We teachers are pretty accustomed to giving feedback, assessment, advice, and sometimes downright criticism. We can dish it out—but can we take it? Dialogue journals offer us a chance to find out. An old friend of ours in Minnesota taught six-week keyboarding classes for many years. For one exercise, she'd have kids write her a formal letter. She always said that "the content doesn't matter as long as you have several paragraphs." Mistake.

Mrs. Charlotte Elm

West Bluff High School

1204 Maple Street

Excelsior, Minnesota, 55397

Dear Mrs. Elm,

So far this semester, the material we have covered has been a bore. We do the same thing every day. I am disappointed with the content of this class. At times I have looked at the clock on your wall, which seems to run backwards, and contemplated suicide.

Despite my utter boredom during this class, I have learned many new keyboarding skills. My rate has gone up considerably since the beginning of the course and my reaches have become easier.

Sincerely yours,

Gil Perez
Gilbert Perez

On a more serious note, a teacher we won't name received the note in Figure 4.21 from a student with special needs.

Thankfully, these kinds of kid notes—and teacher assessment strategies—are very rare.

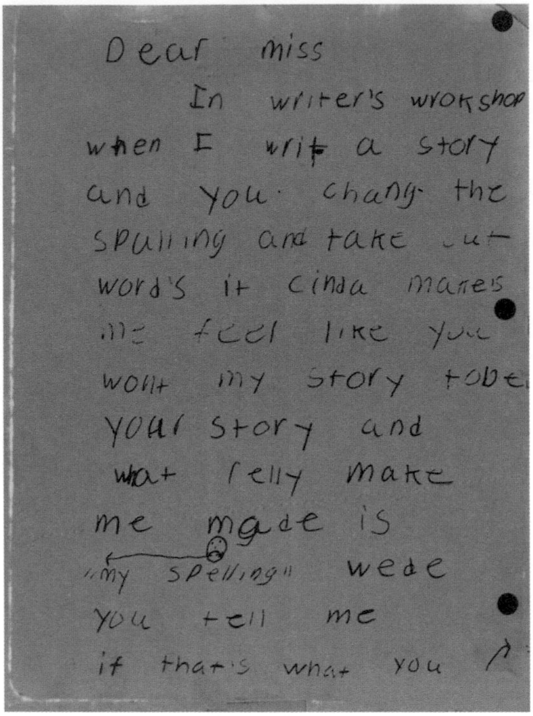

Dear miss
In writer's wrokshop
when I writ a story
and you chang the
spelling and take out
word's it cinda mares
me feel like you
wont my story tobe
your story and
what relly make
me made is
"my spelling" wede
you tell me
if that's what you

Dear Miss . . . , In writer's workshop when I write a story and you change the spelling and take out words it kinda makes me feel like you want my story to be your story and what really makes me mad is "my spelling" ☹ Would you tell me if that's what you think you're doing? Would you like it if someone wanted your story? But you might like it and want to have it but that's not what I think. PS: Would you try and be patient with my spelling.

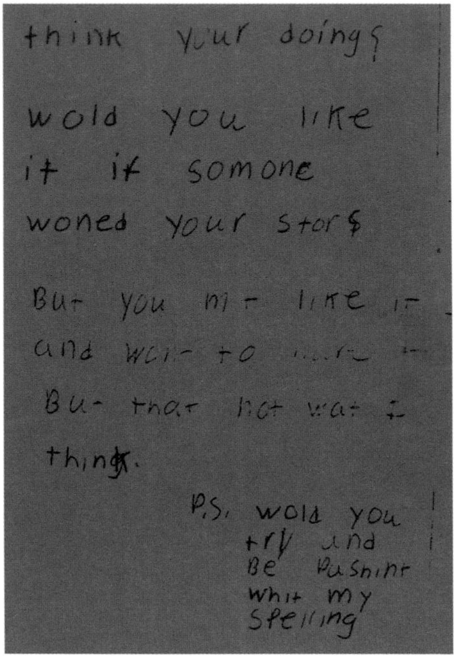

think your doings
wold you like
it if somone
woned your stor
But you
and
think.
P.S. wold you
try and
Be pashint
whit my
spelling

a Turns out this teacher owned a hierarchy of face ink stamps that ran the gamut of assessment from—who knows?—ecstasy to revulsion. And she would slam a big frowny face on every spelling error her fourth graders made, IEP or not.

Figure 4.21

Listening to kids' advice can really pay off—both for the good ideas we get from them, and from the trust that's built when we solicit their feedback and then take it seriously. High school teacher Nancy Steineke asks her kids to offer suggestions for improving their sophomore English class. You can see their ideas reflected in the responses Nancy wrote.

Dear Katie,

I think you are right about getting up more—putting some more physical activity into class. Have you ever seen any good activities that other teachers have used? If so, tell me about them. In any event, if we're just still sitting around two weeks from now, remind me that we need to move!

Mrs. Steineke

Dear Matt,

Thanks for the input on the assignments; I'll keep that "more visual" idea in mind. Since you are enjoying *Band of Brothers,* you might enjoy some other nonfiction books about World War 2. I know of a few, so if you need some suggestions, just ask. BTW, have you read any books by Chris Crutcher? There are a couple of them that focus on a high school swim team. All of his books have something to do with sports.

Mrs. Steineke

Dear Steve,

Almost everyone has mentioned the book buddy project, so I'm definitely going to bring that back soon. I'm glad you've found the text marking useful. This is a strategy you can use in any class any time you have to read something and really think about it. *After* is one of my favorite YA novels as well, but I thought the ending was dumb. Aliens? Come on. It would be better if the new "evil" principal's control motivations were something believable.

Mrs. Steineke

Nancy's undefensive and appreciative responses make a huge statement about what kind of relationship she is seeking with students.

Behavior Support Letters

With all our years in the classroom, we've both had our share of "behavior problems"—and sometimes our students also act up (insert rim-shot here). Of course, when there are immediate, life-threatening misbehaviors, you have to act swiftly to restore order and guarantee the survival of Western civilization. But, when you think about it, how common are those "must act now" scenarios?

For us anyway, the common, garden-variety, drip-drip-drip, death-of-a-thousand-cuts discipline issues are mostly recurrent and low-level. It's kids who do, or don't do, the same damn bothersome thing, day in and day out. But if you call these students out in class, you're putting them on the defensive. Excuses, bad feelings, and ongoing noncompliance are the typical outcomes. And for kids with interfering behaviors, any public rebuke provides an often irresistible opening for a psycho-throwdown, with you playing the other Mexican wrestler.

How about a nice, private, patient, and reasonable letter instead?

> Dear Brad,
>
> Today was the third day in a row that you came to your inquiry group without your research materials and your journal. You know that this bogs down the group and makes progress hard for everyone. People are counting on you to do your share of the work, on time.
>
> So please decide what steps you are going to take to solve this problem and write me back by tomorrow at 8 with your solution. Let me know how I can help you implement your plan.
>
> *Thanks, Mr. Daniels*

> To Daniel and Devin,
>
> We've talked about how distracting it can be for other kids when some people walk around and poke their head into other people's meetings. Take a look at your own group's ground rules: One says "no going to other groups." Write back and tell me how you'll fix this tomorrow.
>
> *Ms. Daniels*

Dear Brynne,

I couldn't help noticing this morning that you seemed sad or distracted. Is there something I can do to help you refocus? Can you come back and dive in with us, as usual? Let me know how to help.

Mr. Daniels

Luke,

Tomorrow, will you please try to put all your things away at cleanup time? Post your answer on the message board when you come in, and I will check in with you to see how it goes.

Thanks,

Mr. D

Raphael,

I notice you have a hard time putting your phone away when we start class. Please find a nice deep pocket and zip it in there!

Mrs. D

One of the advantages of these behavior support notes is you can hand one to a kid at the end of class (or email it after school, even better). Then they can read it in private and be mad at you, and then read it later and be less mad. And then come to terms with the fact that you're asking for a response or a behavior change. We have found that these quick letters are amazingly effective—and are great souvenirs to share with parents as needed.

You might wonder, don't kids get freaked when they're handed a letter at the end of class? And don't the other kids hoot and catcall when they see somebody receiving a teacher note after class? "Oooooh, Brandon's gonna get it!" Actually, if you have a classroom where constant letter-writing is standard behavior, nobody knows what the content of any note might be. As we tell our students at the beginning of a class: "We're all going to write each other a lot of letters in here this year."

The preceding examples are mostly the onetime, fine-tuning variety. We can also engage students in ongoing behavior support dialogues. At a high school in Chicago, one student was consistently disrupting Mack Dillon's algebra class. So Mack and teacher-consultant Yolanda Simmons cooked up a plan to enlist Karen as a classroom helper, instead of rebuking her as a behavior problem. Yolanda initiated a series of letters in which she asked Karen to help her figure out how to improve the math class. Together, they laid a plan, and a couple of weeks later, Karen celebrated her success in "saving" Mr. Dillon.

> Dear Ms. Simmons,
>
> In my opinion, 7th period Algebra has really improved since I wrote Mr. Dillon a few suggestions that I felt would help to improve 7th pd. Algebra.
>
> Mr. Dillon used my advice wisely. He took them and expanded them in many different ways. For example, I suggested that he let people who understood what they were doing, help others who didn't. Mr. Dillon gave the class a quick quiz just to see where we were in the lesson, and to identify those who had the lesson down pat. Mr. Dillon and I place them in groups where they could help others around them. That has been successful.
>
> In class Mr. Dillon doesn't have to do a lot of yelling because the seats are arranged so that the students can do their work without talking to their friends. I even heard a few of my friends in 7th period say that Algebra is going better than before.
>
> In conclusion, I think that Mr. Dillon's 7th pd. Algebra class has really improved thanks to you Ms. Simmons, Mr. Dillon, and myself. So far, all of my suggestions have preserved Mr. Dillon from failure.
>
> *Karen*

Karen, the scourge of seventh period, became a solid citizen through Yolanda's surreptitious behavior support letters. Now that's *discipline*.

Student Self-Assessments

We've already seen the many ways that Michele Timble uses letter-writing with her fourth graders. Sometimes she asks kids to reflect on their work by writing a note to their future selves. Just the salutations hint at the delight kids take in this time-travel experiment:

> Dear myself,
>
> Dear Future Self,
>
> Dear Beautiful,
>
> Dear Noelia in the future,
>
> Dear wonderful awesome self,
>
> Dear Future Me,

Figure 4.22 is Jolie's self-assessment of her work in a small-group research project.

We're betting that Jolie does become a great leader if she can hang onto this self-insight, which most bosses seem to lose along the way!

Kid-Kid Assessments

Just as we want kids to become increasingly responsible for assessing themselves, setting goals, and monitoring their work, we also want them to offer useful feedback to their classmates. But we step carefully here, not wanting any impulsive or hurtful words to get loose in the classroom.

With Michele modeling constructive feedback every day, and the kids having frequent chances to skillfully address an audience in writing, they're ready to give each other some mini assessment notes.

After students presented their findings on some mini research projects, Michele invited kids to send each other brief notes of feedback and suggestions (see Figures 4.23, 4.24, and 4.25).

These comments have a pretty good level of specificity—what worked well and the occasional suggestion. And everyone is now well equipped to talk about President Taft at any future cocktail party.

Dear amazing epical awesome future Self,
Your just about to start another inquiry project! I'm writing this from your first inquiry circle, wow did you do good! I'm going to remind you some things you did good on and also some down hills. Good things, Your art work was amazing and you were a great leader! Down hills, you were a bit bossy words in a while when you were trying to get your team mates to present better, but all in all you did pretty good, please be less bossy but still be a leader!

from,
your Past Self.
(Jolie.)

a Jolie reflects upon her own uphills and "downhills" as an inquiry group member.

Figure 4.22

> Dear Pricilla, I loved your project! There were a ton of interesting facts.
> Love, Katy

Figure 4.23

Figure 4.24

Figure 4.25

But there are other benefits beyond presenter feedback here, too. When you sit down to listen to a classmate's presentation, having this task in mind has a very salutary effect. Classroom audiences are notoriously twitchy and distractible, but if kids know they will be writing a note to each presenter immediately afterwards, it focuses their attention.

"Classroom audiences are notoriously twitchy and distractible, but if kids know they will be writing a note to each presenter immediately afterwards, it focuses their attention."

TEACHER RESPONSE TO STUDENT WRITING

Purpose: When students submit written work to teachers, a powerful way of responding is to write them a letter commenting on the writing.

Given all our warnings about not overdoing the writing of letters to students, this next variation may come as a surprise. We believe that, on occasion, when you have the peace of mind and time, it's great to put down the red pen and respond to kids' writing with—writing. We are so professionally enculturated to point out what's *wrong* with students' writing, but working writers urgently need human validation and feedback on what's working well.

Elaine: Teaching writing in high school or college, I have always written letters. For me, it's the best way to give a whole and thoughtful response to student writing. I have done the occasional rubric, but both the students and I find the letters more satisfying. I write to them on real stationery, and start with "Dear So-and-So." This is a big effort making a handmade "gift" for every student, but it speaks volumes about both craft and caring. My hand gets tired too, so sometimes I will type and print the letters on schoolish stationery templates I've found for free online.

I respond personally to the writing piece, giving examples from my life that relate to what they've written. I talk about the significance of what they've said and suggest how to strengthen their message. I also respond to the style, the voice, and the language, noting all the positives I see. I may also give suggestions or note one or two areas, say quotation marks or apostrophes, where the student needs more work. All in all, the students are able to receive the feedback better in this way, couched in a personal context. It feels profoundly specific. And I love not being constrained by numbers or points.

So, in this way, letters can be for assessment as well as classroom climate development. And as students revise their papers, they write me back, sometimes on stationery, sometimes via email. I treasure those responses. We come to know each other this way.

Abigail,

I just finished rereading your story, and it really does take my breath away. You are a beautiful writer.

Melvin is alive in this book. His boredom and depression are drawn so realistically. By way of connection, I think my son grew up in his room, watching TV with the blinds down. It was a good thing his room was next to the kitchen or I never would have seen him at all, I think. Your colorized photos enhance the story beautifully. I had to pause to really think about them. I think my favorite is the rumpled envelope with the address. Reminds me of letters I've kept, both dear and damaging.

The mom's careworn and stressed situation is presented thoughtfully. The miscommunication between her and Melvin is painful. Words said, heard or not heard, listened to or not. How quickly parents can fall into harping, and how equally quickly kids can fall into brood mode.

The absent dad is a full character, too. Melvin persists that his dad is cool, and maybe he was. But why is it up to the mom to tell Melvin the truth? That's pretty dreadful, not behavior of a good dad. Jerk. And a new baby, a knife in the heart. I'm wondering what in your life caused you to pick this path for the story? I sense you have a good family situation, but I think you must have experienced some grave disappointments to be able to write this so sensitively.

But I haven't even talked about the actual writing yet, and that's what blows me away. Several sentences or images that affect me are:

1. "I hate kidney beans, that weird skin they have."
2. "That's twice this month she's fed the floor before me."
3. "She actually brought me home . . . pink blanket . . ."
4. "I have some important zombie killing to attend to."
5. "the thick tires on the rough pavement"
6. "She makes weird transitions like that all the time."

Pointing out specific words or phrases that worked is more powerful than almost any generalization a teacher can make about a piece of writing.

7. "Final Falls . . . it sounded a lot like my favorite video game . . ."

8. "The picture is so clear you could eat the turkey they advertise at Thanksgiving . . ."

9. "the locked drawer"

10. "Truth. What does that even mean? If you say it enough . . ." Such a great reminder from the earlier: "Tacos. What does that word even mean . . . ?"

I can feel what it's like to be in that house, smell the living room, the ground meat cooking, the fresh laundry. You've done such a remarkable job of creating an environment in so few pages. I know you must have worked so very hard and can't say enough about how much I enjoyed your story. Keep it in a safe place.

Sincerely,
Elaine Daniels

MULTI-AGE DIALOGUE JOURNALS

Purpose: Older kids can be strong writing mentors for younger ones, as well as offering them a big buddy around the school.

When Smokey was teaching sixth grade a few years back, he partnered up with first-grade teacher Jessica Gonzalez to establish yearlong writing buddies. Figure 4.26 is one example of an exchange between sixth grader Karen and Neivy, a first-grade English language learner.

To understand how this conversation was created in April, you have to envision Neivy, in September, a first grader recently arrived from Mexico, sitting in the lap of her very own great big sixth grader, Karen. Carefully teacher-selected pairs of first and sixth graders are scattered around the rug in Jessica's first-grade room at Salazar Elementary School in Santa Fe, New Mexico. Everyone has a brand-new writing buddy; one pair is a match made in heaven—Big Jose and Little Jose.

Because it's early in the year, the little ones cannot write much yet. So the partners are passing one pad back and forth, writing or drawing as best they can, and reading the letters out loud to each other. Some first graders are simply dictating to their sixth graders a letter they would write *if they could*. Later

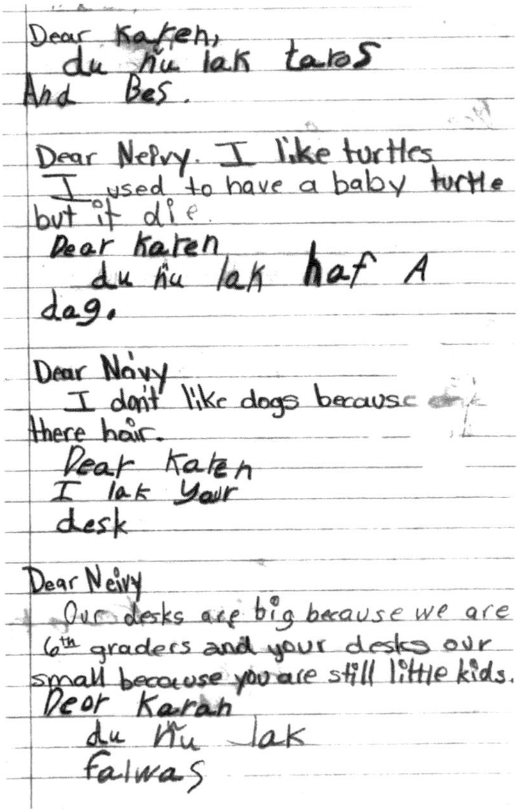
Dear Karen,
du hu lak taros
And Bes.
Dear Nefvy. I like turtles
I used to have a baby turtle
but it die.
Dear Karen
du hu lak haf A
dag.
Dear Navy
I don't like dogs because
there hair.
Dear Katen
I lak Your
desk
Dear Neivy
Our desks are big because we are
6th graders and your desks our
small because you are still little kids.
Deor Karah
du hu lak
falwas

Dear Karen, Do you like turtles and bees?

Dear Neivy, I like turtles. I used to have a baby turtle but it died.

Dear Karen, Do you like have a dog?

Dear Neivy, I don't like dogs because of their hair.

Dear Karen, I like your desk.

Dear Neivy, Our desks are big because we are 6th graders and your desks are small because you are still little kids.

Dear Karen, Do you like flowers?

Figure 4.26 (continued)

Figure 4.26 (continued)

Dear Neivy, I like flowers but my favorite are roses.

Dear Karen, I love flowers, love.

Dear Neivy, What other band besides RBD do you like?

Dear Karen, I don't know how to read.

Dear Neivy, Maybe I can teach you how to read because I'm your friend.

Dear Karen, Yes, love Neivy

a Karen feels the conversation fading and tries to amp it up with a new topic, and her partner responds with a surprising revelation.

Figure 4.26

in the year, they'll be able to compose their own letters and "mail" them to the other end of the building without trooping through the halls to sit side by side.

Karen went on to be a wonderful teacher for Neivy, as they exchanged letters throughout the year, stretching Neivy's sense of herself as a writer. (And Ms. Gonzalez was a pretty good teacher, too.) All through the year, whenever they saw their sixth-grade buddies in the halls or at an assembly—or, oh my God, at the grocery store!—the first graders felt 6 feet tall.

As the year came toward a close at Salazar, a K–6 school, the sixth-grade writing buddies would be heading off to middle school. No! A big graduation ceremony was planned, and the first graders asked to be part of it. At the June graduation ceremony, with a full house of families dressed in their finest, the first-grade writing buddies took the stage last. With great ceremony, the now 7-year-olds each presented their beloved sixth-grade pals with one last special letter, placed in a painstakingly decorated envelope. Inside each one is advice on how to succeed in middle school.

Figure 4.27

In this chapter, we have seen dialogue journals in which kids criticize the teacher's handwriting, reflect on their own social skills, work through math problems, give advice to older students, and much more. This range of use shows the power of paired written conversations. When we sit down to write with just one partner, we enter a relationship with complete accountability, one to another. Not only do we "cover" curricular topics, we also build trusting relationships between teachers and students, between kids and kids, and between big kids and little kids.

MANAGEMENT TIPS FOR DIALOGUE JOURNALS

Training Students. As with any new classroom activity, it is vital that the teacher demonstrate it first. You can pass out samples of yourself corresponding with another teacher or a volunteer student. Better yet, do it live in the classroom by projecting both partners at work writing or composing on side-by-side easel charts, exchanging places to "receive" and answer each letter.

Forming Partners. If it helps, feel free to match kids up for optimum results—especially when they are first trying this structure. In pairing kids, consider text production; some kids were born with a golden shovel in their hands, and can churn out text without hesitation. Others just write more slowly, maybe because they are actually trying to think before they write. Since it can be discouraging to be partnered with someone who writes way more and way faster, we may pair kids by writing speed. This is temporary grouping, not labeling. Over time, kids should be writing with lots of different partners.

Using Effective Prompts. On pages 66–69, we have listed a variety of general and specific prompts for written conversations. Some are quite open-ended, simply calling for students to share reactions, responses, interpretations, opinions, wonderings, or summaries of the text, topic, or experience that's under study. Other prompts can be highly focused, yet still invite original responses when they focus on *why* or *how*, not so much on *who/what/where/when*. Factual recall questions do not spark conversations. We must give kids something rich, complex, and multidimensional to write about. There's always a temptation to infuse a quiz or a reading check into our prompts, but doing so usually kills off the conversational impulse.

Dealing With Uneven Numbers. The great thing about pair work is there can only be *one* straggler in any classroom (unless you let kids immediately form groups of three, which you never would). If there is a "leftover" student, either you be his or her partner or else allow *a single* group of three to work together.

Timing the Writing. For the "live" notes, which pairs write in class, we want to keep the pace up, so allow *one to three minutes* of writing, or something like *a quarter to half a page* between passes. For the "takeaway" dialogue journals, which are composed more thoughtfully and sent like mail, kids might write for *five or more minutes*, filling a *full page*, sometimes more.

Sore Hands. American students (and their teachers) do far less handwriting these days, so we are all out of shape for extended old-school writing. We can bemoan the death of cursive, but this is a reality. Two solutions: First, build kids' stamina by starting short and ramping up. Writing by hand is a life skill that's far from obsolete. Second option, do the writing on a keyboard—if everyone is on the same type of device. See the following tip.

Using Technology. We say much more about this in Chapter 6, but of course you can have kids write dialogue journals on computers, laptops, tablets, or even phones—as long as everyone is using the same tool and can use it as fluently as a pen or pencil. Many teachers use a web space (Edmodo, Google Docs) where they can arrange kids into partnerships or "rooms" for one-to-one dialoguing. But remember that traditional paper-and-pencil, sitting-beside-each-other written conversation has some special benefits. For one, you can look right up in an instant and switch to talking out loud.

The Teacher's Role During Dialogue Journals. When kids are working on dialogue journals, your job is to keep moving and keep time. You are looking over the pairs' shoulders, watching the writing go down on the page, perhaps stopping to whisper some help or encouragement—and calling the letter swaps at intervals that make sense. Enjoy how hard the kids are working!

Moving Toward Kids' Choosing Partners. Especially early in the year, it is healthy to have kids *randomly* assigned to partners, with those pairings changing very frequently, so that everyone gets to work with everyone else. Then, once we have built strong and diffuse friendship patterns throughout the group (by Thanksgiving? by second semester?), we can let kids pick their own partners.

English Language Learners and Students With Special Needs. If we have English language learners, it can help for them to work with a student from the same language group. And we always encourage *drawing* as a way to participate in a written conversation. But even when working in English, the rehearsal time kids get in written conversations (versus having to spontaneously speak in front of a whole class) is an accommodation in itself.

The Assessment of Written Conversations

One of the great features of written conversations is that they offer us rich opportunities to assess kids' thinking, content knowledge, expression, and interaction. Unlike out-loud discussions that vanish into the void, these letters can be collected, saved, studied, and assessed.

But. But. We do not grade written conversations for grammar, usage, and mechanics. Though it can be devilishly hard, we must restrain that itchy trigger finger on the red pen. These letters are by definition *rough drafts*. While they are being composed and swapped, there is no time given for corrections and edits—the conversation moves too fast for that, and it should. These are thinking exercises, not editing drills.

It can be hard to lay off marking those errors. For one thing, we teachers ar e really good at finding kids' mistakes, and it's in our DNA not to let them slide. But if we try to push proofreading into a spontaneous conversation, we kill the conversation. The effective assessment of writing is all about the occasion and the purpose. As the Common Core makes clear, when we submit kids' best writing to rigorous assessment, they need to have put that writing through multiple steps of careful revision, editing, and polishing. In these written conversations, we are not providing that time or focus. Still, these letters often do provide kids with kernels, seed ideas that can later be developed into extended formal essays or reports.

Similarly, in our hunger to be sure students have good written discussions, we may be tempted to feed them preapproved discussion questions, developed by us. Where's the rigor in that? In written conversations, we want students to *take full responsibility for an academic conversation*. Holding high standards does not mean keeping kids on "intellectual welfare," always feeding them a topic. Bah! Make the kids do the work themselves: require *them* to find topic worth consideration, dig deeply into it, make sound arguments, stay focused, build on others' ideas, dig out of dead ends, and find a new subject if this one peters out. Now that's rigor.

SCORING RUBRIC FOR WRITTEN CONVERSATIONS

Trait	C	S	R	NA	Notes
Has prepared for the discussion by reading, viewing, or researching					
Joins fully in conversation with substantial and sustained entries					
Responds directly to partners' relevant comments or questions					
Supports own views with evidence from the text/content/experience					
Digs below the surface of subject matter to develop new ideas and fresh interpretations					
Poses questions that advance the discussion					
Disagrees agreeably and specifically					
Builds on other members' ideas					
Stays focused on topic and observes timing					
Invites and acknowledges others' contributions					
Uses a respectful and inclusive tone					

C = Consistently; S = Sometimes; R = Rarely; NA - Not applicable

Write-Arounds

Dear Reader,

In this version of written conversation, all the advantages of silent discussion coalesce. Small groups of kids write and exchange notes about a curricular topic for several rounds—maybe 5 to 15 minutes of sustained writing— and then they burst into out-loud talk that's rooted in their extended written rehearsals.

Smokey and Elaine

DEFINITION: Three to five students, sitting side by side, writing notes to each other, serially exchanging these notes, commenting and building upon each other's ideas. This shift from paired dialogue journals is more than just adding a couple more people to the conversation. Extended write-arounds invite deeper thinking, encourage lively debate, and release tremendous energy. Typically, after three or four notes have been exchanged, we have kids shift to out-loud conversation in their groups, and finally join in short but energetic and well-informed whole-class discussions.

"This is more than just adding a couple more people to the conversation. Extended write-arounds invite deeper thinking, encourage lively debate, and release tremendous energy."

VARIATIONS:

- Drawn Conversations
- Silent Literature Circles
- Content-Area Write-Arounds
- Text on Text

ORIGINS: Unlike one-to-one dialogue journals, we cannot award any one educator credit for having invented multiperson "live" letter-writing. Write-arounds have probably been with us since letter-writing was invented. But Toby Fulwiler of the University of Vermont definitely drew attention to this strategy in *The Letter Book* (2000). Though the book was aimed at college teachers, and all the samples were of university students' writing, some members of the National Writing Project saw the value in these multiperson exchanges, and brought the idea to K–12 education. For what it's worth, we have been trying to popularize this strategy for a long time, in books like *Content-Area Writing, Subjects Matter, Mini-Lessons for Literature Circles,* and *Texts and Lessons for Content-Area Reading.*

"Offer students a thought-provoking topic to invite their best thinking, coach them on how to write steadily and silently, and make use of the students' ideas in subsequent discussions."

QUICK LOOK:

Maggie Borland's juniors are reading J. D. Salinger's classic *Catcher in the Rye.* Maggie has put students in four-member write-around groups to have thoughtful written discussions of the book as it unfolds. And these are supposed to be more than simple "loved it" or "hated it" conversations. Maggie always offers students a thought-provoking topic to invite their best thinking, coaches them on how to write steadily and silently, makes use of the students' ideas in subsequent discussions, and collects the papers when the lesson is done.

As kids complete Chapter 9, Maggie invites groups to in engage in another series of written discussions. Each student gets out a full-size piece of paper and puts their initials—their personal "check-in"—in the left-hand margin. Maggie provides a very focused topic: Holden Caulfield's attitudes toward sex, as they are being revealed in this pivotal chapter. She sets kids writing, allows about one minute each, and tells kids when to pass their notes. The whole thing takes about

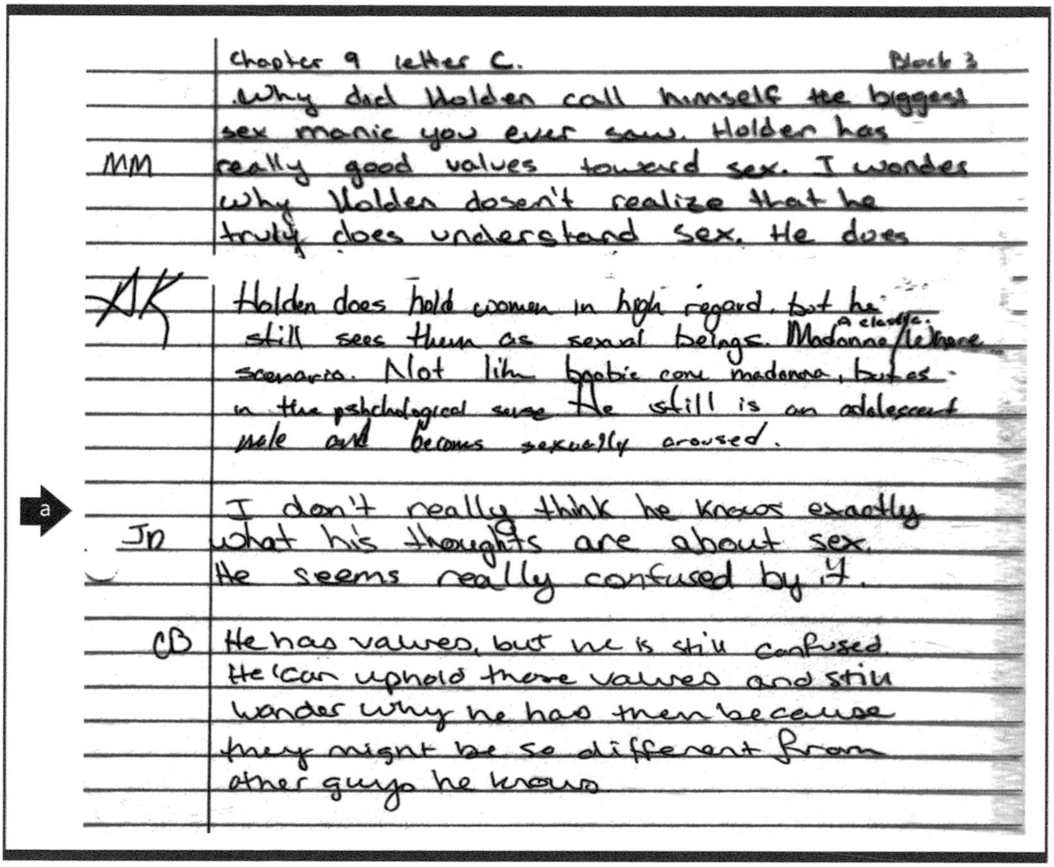
Chapter 9 letter C. Block 3

MM Why did Holden call himself the biggest sex manic you ever saw. Holden has really good values toward sex. I wonder why Holden dosen't realize that he truly does understand sex. He does

AK Holden does hold women in high regard, but he still sees them as sexual beings. A classic Madonna/Whore scenario. Not like boobie cone madonna, but as in the pshchological sense. He still is an adolescent male and becomes sexually aroused.

a

JD I don't really think he knows exactly what his thoughts are about sex. He seems really confused by it.

CB He has values, but he is still confused. He can uphold those values and still wander why he has them because they might be so different from other guys he knows

a

This quick conversation illustrates a pattern we often see in write-arounds: the deepening of thinking through discussion. The early comments here are general and not well grounded in the book's themes. But when JD checks in, and pushes off from the previous comments, the thinking gets closer to the meat of the book, and then CB arguably hits it out of the park. Four heads are often better than one—but not instantly.

Figure 5.1

five minutes. Figure 5.1 on the previous page shows one of the four discussion sheets that one group created.

With the fourth pass, kids receive back the letter they started, with the other three kids' comments added. At this point, Maggie asks everyone to read that page and then circle "the one most interesting sentence" that anyone wrote on the topic. Then she invites groups to continue their conversation aloud, using the circled sentences as discussion starters. After groups have talked for another three or four minutes, Maggie calls everyone back for a whole-class discussion. Hands fly up. It's the opposite of the typical whole-class discussion where a few volunteer and the majority sleep. Here, it seems like everyone—even the usually shy kids—wants to throw in an idea, to join in the wider conversation. And that's because everyone has had a chance to think, rehearse, and try out his or her ideas with others, before being asked to risk wider disclosure.

> "It's the opposite of the typical whole-class discussion where a few volunteer and the majority sleep."

LAUNCHING LESSON:

The New Mexico state curriculum guide requires that middle school kids learn about the rule of law, how laws are made, and—like all states—the U.S. Constitution. So when Smokey was teaching sixth grade in Santa Fe, he developed a lesson for this unit around the issue of outlawing "dangerous dogs."

Smokey: Whenever you are starting a unit about ideas that seem abstract or distant from the kids (such as the legal system), you need to hook them with something up close and personal. I have always been struck by the study done by Ivey and Broaddus in 2007, which showed that the most effective teachers begin units with the most lively, relevant, even gut-wrenching aspects of a required topic—and then work kids back to the core concepts. In other words, when you are beginning a unit of study, engagement trumps everything.

> "The most effective teachers begin units with the most lively, relevant, even gut-wrenching aspects of a required topic—and then work kids back to the core concepts."

So, the rule of law. How to begin? I was aware of a growing national controversy about pit bull dogs and the extra level of danger they allegedly pose to the public. This belief has led to a proliferation of "breed-specific laws," controlling the conditions of ownership of some dogs, but not others. I also know that pit bulls are especially popular here in New Mexico; some kids in my class have one at home. And our daily papers often carry stories about dog attacks, mostly in poorer neighborhoods. So I built my rule of law launching lesson around dog laws.

To begin, I created a PowerPoint of dog images starting with adorable puppies and working its way up to fierce-looking pit bulls. Google images also offered plenty of hospital photos of chewed-up victims, which I avoided. Finally I downloaded several one-page articles—pro, con, and neutral—about breed-specific laws.

Then I provided some instructions:

> All right, guys. We're starting a new unit today, and to begin, I've got some pictures to show you. While I go through these, feel free to talk out loud, to your partner or to the screen, about what you are seeing, what you wonder, what reactions you have. OK?
>
> *Now I run the series of dog photos with little narration. Kids make oooing noises over the cute puppies. They laugh at pictures of people playing with their dog— throwing Frisbees, swimming, and even one German shepherd skydiving with its owner. Kids are touched by photos of dogs helping handicapped humans. Then, when we finally come to photos of several scary dogs, dogs fighting with each other, and dogs menacing humans, there's quiet.*
>
> Turn to your partner and talk. Have you ever been bitten or threatened by a dog? Go ahead and talk. *After a couple of minutes, I call the kids back together. There are plenty of hands in the air, and kids are eager to tell their stories of both minor and harrowing dog encounters. Some point out scars on their bodies.*
>
> You know, some places in the USA and other countries have made certain breeds of dogs *illegal* to buy or sell. That means once those dogs die, their owners can never get another one of that breed. *Now, I project a summary of Ontario's pit bull ban (Ontario Ministry of the Attorney General, 2004), and we read through it together. Some kids are shocked to hear that these Canadian pets must be sterilized, can never be bred, cannot be sold or traded, and must wear a muzzle and be on a short leash when in public. There's a mixture of outrage, support, and puzzlement.*

I can tell you are really curious and would like to know more about this issue. So, today I have brought you five different articles about pit bulls, dog attacks, and breed-specific laws. *I quickly recount the choices.*

"Pit Bulls Are Inherently Dangerous Animals, Maryland Court Says"

"Study Confirms Breed Bans Don't Work"

"Own a Pit Bull? Good Luck Renting an Apartment"

"6 Reasons Pit Bulls Make Great Pets"

"Man Loses Foot in Pit Bull Attack on Beach"

I want you to choose the article that you are most interested in and read it. Then we'll get in our table groups of four or five, and have a written discussion, OK?

But first, we need to decide how to annotate these articles. When we are reading nonfiction, we always "stop, think, and act," right? We notice what's going on in our minds, and we leave tracks of our thinking we can use to support us later when we talk or write about it.

For these articles, we're going to annotate using "PCQ." What's that? I just made it up! Here's what I mean.

P is for Pro. When you are reading your chosen article and you run across a part that makes you feel you are FOR breed-specific laws, put a big P in the margin and write some words to help you remember your thinking.

C is for Con. When you are reading your chosen article and you run across some information that makes you feel you are AGAINST breed-specific laws, put a big C in the margin and write some words to help you remember your thinking.

Q is for Question. When you are reading your chosen article and you run across some information that makes you have a QUESTION about breed-specific laws, put a big Q in the margin and write some words to help you remember your thinking.

Now I allow time for students to read and annotate. For kids who finish early, we have the norm that you either reread or move on to another article. When kids are done reading and note-taking and are seated in their table groups, I reiterate the directions for a write-around discussion.

OK, guys, we have done this plenty of times before. We are going to discuss today's topic not by taking turns out loud, but by writing simultaneous notes to each other and passing them around the group every couple of minutes. So take out a full-size sheet of paper and put your name in the upper left-hand margin. This is your check-in, and every time a paper is passed to you, you'll sign your name before you write anything.

OK, let me frame the topic and you can get started "talking." What are your thoughts about these breed-specific laws? Do you think they are fair? Right? A good idea? What are some pros and cons that you annotated, or some questions you had? Use your annotations however they help you to keep the conversation going. So go ahead now, take two minutes and write a note to your group about dangerous dogs and breed-specific laws. I'll let you know when there is 15 seconds left.

I patrol the room, managing the writing and passing process, as outlined on pages 168–169. I have kids write and pass three times inside each group, which takes around 10 minutes; I am giving them about two to three minutes of writing time for each letter.

Now that there is plenty on the pages, I have kids shift to out-loud talk at their tables for about three minutes, and then we move to a whole-class discussion. Now practically every kid, shy or talky, wants to get their voice heard. There's none of the usual "pulling teeth" to get volunteers to raise their hands and talk. I can also call on any student, because I know they've had plenty of rehearsal time— and they have their own words written down, right in front of them to draw upon.

> *"Now practically every kid, shy or talky, wants to get their voice heard. There's none of the usual 'pulling teeth' to get volunteers to raise their hands and talk."*

Here is sampling of the dog discussion from two different groups.

Group I

Written Conversation
Oct. 12 2011
303

Dog Laws

I think there are both bad dogs & bad owners. It might not be the owners' fault, in all cases. I think we do need some laws like for dangerous dogs, like don't abandon a pitbull, but the dog shouldn't be put down if he bit someone. That should depend on the severity of the case. What I think should happen is that owners should have a liscence, or have to be trained to own a pitbull.

D.S.

I agree! Pitbulls should NOT be put down if they attack. We do need a law for super dangerous ▬▬ dogs but not all Pitbulls bite! There are bad dogs & bad owners. Some dogs are really bad but some are like that because of owners. If you want a Pitbull you should be trained though. They can be vevy agressive if provoked.

J.A
I agree as well. Pit buts shouldn't be treated wrong because they did something bad to someone. It can also be the owners fault because sometimes the way the owners act around their dogs is how the dogs are ended up being. You should always be trained before getting a pitbull because it is big *responsibility to take care of a pitbull. Let me tell you that in the article I was reading. it stated that a girl was running away from a pitbull since it looked like he was going to kill her. So she was bitten on the Floor.

C.B
The dog did nothing I mean nothing of the world. Pitbulls and rottwellers been in my article and they been in shelters not living in good homes but in horrible homes. Sometimes I re-love dogs and sometimes not.

After the written discussion, I asked kids to star "the one most interesting sentence" that came up in the conversation, and to use these sentences to start an out-loud conversation.

Figure 5.2

Group 2

① Dog laws

→ a

A.R. I thought it was horrible, the way they treated the dogs. Just because of there apperence. I think there should be liberty and justice for all dogs. And cruell people should be muzzled up and have certain rules. And I'm wondering is why pit bulls. Why not other dogs? Why not bankers for their rames? Why not other big dogs?

L.R. I think you are right. what about other dogs? what if they bite or cause harm? Even if the dog looks tiny and harmless but it could do alot. I would connect this to what happened to me when I got bit by a tiny harmful dog. It left blood and a bruise. Pit bulls should be treated the same as other dogs, as a matter of fact why not other dogs be muzzled or killed for their appearence. All dogs should have the same rights and at least ①

have the same amount of freedom that other types of dogs should have.

C.C: In Respons to A.R. and L.R.. I would agree to what you guys said what about German Sheperds and other bigger or thicker dogs. L.R. is correct even the smallest, cutest, and/or most harmless looking dog/s could harm people. Dogs Dogs should have equal rights. This reminds me of the Civil Rights Movement here in th U.S. dogs don't have equal rights.

G.C To Respond to A.R and L.R and C.C I agree with all of you! Because I have Met Some of the nicest pitbulls in the past! When I was 7 I got bit by the smallest ②

→ a AR read about how dangerous dogs have often been abused by their owners. Why not muzzles for cruel *people*, he reasons.

Figure 5.3 (continued)

Figure 5.3 (continued)

dog you have ever seen. The scar is still on my finger. There was so much blood and tears. It hurt so much. My father works with animal care and last week I went to his office and read about 2 German Shepards that went around the block killing other dogs, biting people. But then again they were abandoned. No owner and the back yard was full of feces and flyes and it was horrible. Worse thing I have ever seen.

 Ouch! Talk about bringing personal connections to our reading. And yet see how GC maintains her sympathy for even the big scary German shepherds.

Figure 5.3

In general, these notes show good factual recall from the readings, the relevant use of personal connections, a personal engagement with the topic, and a quest for workable and principled solutions.

DRAWN CONVERSATIONS

Purpose: Invites students to move beyond words only, and use graphic elements in responding to curricular topics.

Drawing is a vital option in all write-arounds. Sometimes the best way to express a thought or a reaction is not with words, but with a quick sketch, cartoon, stick figure scene, flow chart, or diagram. Think of how often in our own lives we resort to graphics (happy/unhappy faces, etc.) to make pungent points. For many kids, up to and including some teenagers, drawing can be their "lead strategy," a bridge that gets them ready to write words. Further, drawing may be a *main* way that younger students, or those with special needs, or those learning a new language, can join in these written discussions. So it is vital that

we officially welcome drawing into write-arounds, so kids know this is a resource for all thinkers, not just for students who struggle. Of course, the best way to make this clear is to model *ourselves* using drawn responses to a text or a topic.

"Drawing may be a main *way that younger students, or those with special needs, or those learning a new language, can join in these written discussions."*

You do not have to be able to write (or read) to join in a write-around! Cheryl Hamilton, who teaches first grade in rural Alberta, read her class a book about playground games. Then she gave them large sheets of paper and invited groups of four kids to have a write-around discussion of the book, using drawings. Each child chose their own color of marker so everyone would know who drew what.

Cheryl allowed about three or four minutes between passes, so this "drawn discussion" occupied a leisurely 15 minutes. (The kids would happily have used even more time drawing.) As the papers traveled around the groups, each student added details to the previous kids' drawings, much as older kids build upon each other's ideas in words.

Beau started with a blank piece of paper, filling most of the page with a magnificent dream playground apparatus—in brown. Then he passed his paper to Emma, who added the three green trees, a stick figure kid standing at the bottom of the slide, and a nice green sun. Then Luke received the picture and added in a blue sky, carefully working around Emma's sun and Beau's signature. When the paper got to Tejah, there wasn't much room left, but she found a spot for another monkey bar, low beneath Beau's mega structure (see Figure 5.4).

With older kids, we often like write-arounds to be silent, but here that rule needn't apply. There's a natural flow between drawing and talk as the kids

Figure 5.4

work side by side. Cheryl circulates through the room, answering questions and coaching: "Remember to save some space for your friends," she advises. She's not shy to interrupt kids for a minute to add suggestions. "If you want to add any words to your picture, you can do that, too. Remember how we talked about labels and captions, talk balloons and thought balloons? Maybe your drawing needs some of those."

Figure 5.5 shows a more even-steven distribution of space. Luke starts it off in the upper left corner with some kids walking, on a fence, maybe? Then Beau comes along with a new playground idea—a baseball field. Following Cheryl's suggestion, he has added some text, labeling first, second, third, fourth (!), and home bases. He then places a shortstop between third and fourth. Before the next pass is called, Luke reaches in and adds a batter and a ball and what looks like a first-base coach. Now it's Emma's turn, and in the upper right she draws some hanging bars with three kids gloriously swinging. Finally Tejah, perhaps inspired by Emma's acrobats, draws a girl with a talk balloon saying, "Wheee!"

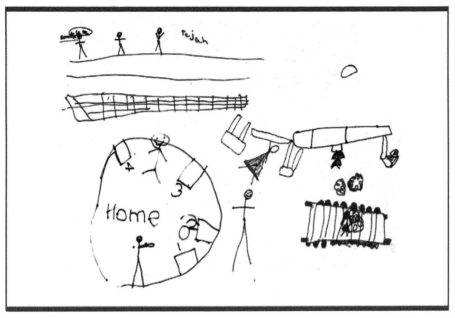

Figure 5.5

SILENT LITERATURE CIRCLES

Purpose: When literature circles happen in writing, everyone gets equal air-time, there are no interruptions, and shy kids are emboldened to take a stance.

In 1994, Smokey wrote one of the first professional books about literature circles, peer-led student book clubs modeled on the voluntary reading groups enjoyed by many grown-ups in their living rooms. Since that time, it's estimated that several million U.S. students have engaged in some variant of this book club model, with small groups of kids (usually four or five) choosing a book they want to read (usually a novel or chapter book) and meeting periodically on their way through the book to talk about it with friends.

Over the 20 years since, countless variations of book clubs have been developed—but none has been more significant than silent literature circles. Since you are halfway through this book, you'll immediately infer that "silent" refers to kids conducting their periodic book club meetings *in writing* instead of out loud. You can imagine how that would work: Groups come to class having read an agreed-upon section of the book, and having made notes in the margins or on Post-its about what they'd like to discuss with their friends—responses and reactions, plot developments, character traits, emerging themes, confusions, and puzzlements.

GENERAL INSTRUCTIONS FOR A WRITE-AROUND

Below are instructions for write-arounds as we tell them to kids:

- Form a group of three or four, pull your seats together, and introduce yourselves (or discuss the assigned warm-up question). *Do not allow twos or fives; push for as many groups of three or four as you can get.*

- Each person please get a large blank piece of paper ready to use. Put your first name in the upper left-hand margin.

- As we work, please follow these rules:

1. Use your best handwriting so friends can read your note.

2. Use all the time I give you for writing. Keep that pen moving until I tell you to exchange papers.

3. No talking. This is a silent activity.

- Ready? OK. We are going to write for just a minute or two. Write your thoughts, reactions, questions, or feelings about our topic. You can address your note to the kids in your group, "Dear Friends," "Dear Buddies," or by names. *The topic can be any common experience: a story, poem, nonfiction article, lab experiment, or textbook selection. If you want to be sure that all kids get started writing promptly, you may decide to project four or five possible "safety net" starter stems (e.g., "One thing I am wondering is ____"), but remove these after the first note-passing. Keep time not by exact minutes and seconds, but by walking and watching kids write. When most students have filled a quarter of a page, it is time to pass.*

- Pass your papers to the left. *Here the teacher reiterates instructions by saying:* Now read the note from your buddy, and just beneath it, write them back for one minute. You can tell your reaction, make a comment, ask questions, share a connection you've made, agree or disagree, or raise a whole new idea. Just keep the conversation going!

Walk the room, looking over shoulders to get the timing right.

- Pass again, please. *Reiterate the instructions if needed, especially about using all the time for writing and working silently, for now.*

Repeat and continue. Trade three times, total. If there are mixed group sizes, no problem—the threes and the fours will still do three trades. Important: You need to allow a little more time with each entry because kids will have more to read with each successive exchange. Mention this when you do it. Again, don't time this activity by actual minutes, but by watching how kids are coming and by calling "Pass" only when most people have written at least a few lines.

- Now pass one last time so that everyone gets back the letter you began with, with your comments at the top. Now read the whole page over and enjoy the conversation that *you* started. You won't write an answer this time.

As soon as kids are done reading and start talking—and they will—say:

- OK. We are going to switch to out-loud talk in just a minute. But to be sure we will have plenty to discuss, I want you to do one more thing. Look through the page you are holding and underline the one most interesting sentence that anyone wrote. Look for something that would be really interesting to discuss further in the group. Ready? OK, the person with the coolest shoes (earliest birthday, etc.) starts it off by reading his or her chosen sentence. Now continue the conversation out loud for a few minutes, using those sentences to support the conversation if you need them.

Option: At this point, you could also announce a more focused prompt ("Do you think that blacklisting could ever happen again in America? Why or why not?") and send kids back into their now warmed-up groups to discuss it.

- Let's gather as a whole class and see where this write-around took us. Will each group please share one highlight, one thread of their discussion? Something you spent time on, something that sparked lively discussion, maybe something you argued about or laughed about. Who'd like to share? *And here's the beauty part—there will be plenty of volunteers.*

Don't forget that you now have two things to discuss—the topic you've just dug into and the process the kids have just used. It is important to reflect upon the activity itself, because you want this write-around tool to enter your kids' repertoires for repeated use.

- Let's discuss this process. What worked for you? How could we make it even better next time? Jot down those ideas and save them for the next write-around.

When the different literature circles sit down together, instead of launching into talk and taking turns speaking out loud, they initiate the conversation by everyone silently writing for two or three minutes. Drawing on their reading notes, each student creates a letter to the group about this section of the book. Then, all students simultaneously pass their notes to the next person in the group, who reads and responds in writing. This written discussion goes on for three or four rounds, maybe 10 or 15 minutes. Next, kids get back the note they started and silently read the whole conversation they provoked. Finally, each group breaks into out-loud conversation, using all their letters (and perhaps a teacher prompt as well) as springboards to further discussion.

This variant of book club discussion works especially well at making space for shy or introverted members, preventing interruptions and off-task distractions, allowing think time, and leaving a tangible artifact of kids' thinking. And this doesn't just work with novels. These days, we have silent literature circle discussions about a whole variety of literary works—including poems, plays, and short stories. You don't need a thick book to have peer-led reading discussion groups!

In Figure 5.6, kids are having a silent literature circle about a two-page memoir piece by Jesus Colon, called "Little Things Are Big." In this unique selection from the 1950s, Colon, a black Puerto Rican, encounters a woman and her three children struggling through a subway station after midnight. Most of the story is Colon's internal dialogue about whether to offer his assistance to the woman who, he can foresee, will have great difficulty making it up the long stairs with her kids and a suitcase. "Courtesy is important to us Puerto Ricans," he reflects. And yet, Colon fears her reaction if he approaches; she might mistake him for a threat and cause a scene.

To energize her students' silent lit circles, teacher Sara Ahmed has withheld the end of the story; the last line they see says "I hesitated." Now, students have to look for clues or evidence in the text that might predict how the story ends. Does he help the woman or not?

We kind of hate to tell you this: In the end, Colon walks by the woman without offering his help. But the point of the memoir is his lifelong regret over that choice. If a similar situation ever happened again, Colon swears, "I will have my

①

Dear Tanya,
I think Jesus is going to risk it.
He's just going to tell himself, at least
I offered to help, if she accepts she
accepts. If she doesn't she doesn't.
I'm just still not sure what she's
going to do though I think first
she might be frightened, I mean
I would too but then maybe
she'll be like ok. I don't know

 a

As Kayla testifies, this is a truly puzzling dilemma.

②

Dear Kayla,
I agree with what you said.
That's how I feel in a lot of
situations. Like I offered my
help, do what you want with it
still, I really hope she doesn't
get offended because Jesus
has good intentions.
Also, I understand what you
said about how you would
feel. I take the CTA and you

have to be careful with
who you trust, because some
people do have bad
intentions. It is hard
trying to not be judge-
mental while keeping
yourself safe. I think that
what Colon's dealing
with.
XOXO ☺,
Tanya

 b

As a daily rider of the Chicago Transit Authority, Tanya knows a thing or two about monitoring your fellow riders on the subway.

③

Well the first thing I wanna
say is I think she's there so late
because thats when her abusive husband
was out getting some drinks and the
lady wanted to leave before he came
back to abuse her and their children
again. I think in the long run he
will help her because he knows
it's the right thing to do no matter
what.
                    Love,
                    Vanessa

c

Vanessa is hypothesizing completely outside the story here, but her inferences match the text perfectly: Why would a woman be in the subway late at night with her kids and as many belongings as she could carry? Most likely, she is running from someone or something.

Figure 5.6 (continued)

Figure 5.6 (continued)

④

> Dear Vanessa,
> I agree with with you
> I mean it is the right thing
> to do when you see someone in
> need. So I agree but one thing
> is that there could be nothing
> wrong with help.
> ♡ -Alyciah

⑤

d

> I think Jesus will probably
> try to help her, even though
> he knows what her most
> probable reaction is. He did
> talk a little about how courtesy
> means a lot to him. Still, in
> that time period, it is a
> risk.

e

> This is why I think he'll
> be an upstander, because he
> seems to be willing to take a
> risk to help someone else.
> Sincerely,
> Tanya

d Tanya sums things up. She recognizes that during the time period of the story, racial tensions were closer to the surface, and that this may help us understand Colon's reticence.

e "Upstander" is a term that labels the choice we have when encountering discrimination; we can be bystanders or upstanders, complicit or activist. Sara's kids have learned this language from the social justice organization Facing History and Ourselves.

⑥

> yeah I agree, he did say that so
> he probably is just going to risk it
> and see what happens. It's probably
> really scary for him because he doesn't
> know how she's going to react but

f

> at the same time, it's going to be
> scary for her too because he's a
> stranger to her and it's late at
> night and dark out who wouldn't
> be scared if a man came to
> you that time at night and offered
> you help and you don't know him.
> What do you think?
> XOXO !!

f The kids have reviewed the text thoroughly, but the puzzle remains. This moment in the subway could be a scary encounter for either of the two participants. It could go either way.

Figure 5.6

courtesy with me," and do the right thing. Meanwhile, Sara's kids have had an energizing silent literature circle around the author's dilemma. And now, as they continue their study of the civil rights movement, they bring a deeper under-standing of those times and their tensions.

CONTENT-AREA WRITE-AROUNDS

Purpose: We can use multistudent written con-versations to engage kids in any subject matter across the curriculum.

Social Studies

As the previous examples suggest, we often use write-arounds to help kids discuss fiction or nonfic-tion texts they've read—or, with the little ones, text we have read aloud to them. But we can also have a write-around about *any other* shared experience— watching a video, doing a science experiment, or conducting an inquiry project.

The history lesson we'll recount shortly was about all the different forms of "battle fatigue," "shell shock," "soldier's heart," and what we now call post-traumatic stress disorder that have been reported throughout the history of war. Each student chose one of six different one-page articles to read and then joined in write-around groups of four to share their new learning and personal responses.

Now, we are going to look at all *four discussions* that happened between Jacob, Lindsey, Laveyn, and Ashley. Four? Here we come to one of the pleasing com-plexities of written discussions: There are as many conversations happening as there are pieces of paper floating around. Let's think this through, step by step.

When a write-around begins, each student has a blank sheet of paper. Then, each person writes for a minute or two, sharing some thoughts or responses to the topic. Then the notes pass to the next person, who is constrained, more or less, to talk about what the first person wrote. And, a few minutes later, a third person receives that sheet of paper, and is invited into that ongoing discussion. So each piece of paper generally carries a different topic with it. Of course, students may change the topic along the way, and the other letters circulating through the group tend to influence what gets written afterwards. So, sometimes, there is a thematic convergence in the later rounds of writing.

Watch how this dynamic unfolds in the following, with a group of four kids from Sheridan High School in Sheridan, Arkansas, *who have never done a written conversation before.* (Because the kids wrote just three entries, not every one appears on each page.)

Paper #1, started by Jacob

Jacob
Byrns

Dear somebody,

Hello, I liked my letter, even though it was graphic. I wish letters/articals were more like that. This PTSD sounds pretty serious, and I think it would help if letters like these were out in the paper we need to understand. Bye!

LO: I agree with Byrns. More people do need to be informed about PTSD because before today, I didn't know much about it either. If many people are being affected by PTSD, shouldn't everyone be informed and try to help people with it? We need to get informed also to know they symptoms to see if we know anyone with it.

LJ: I agree with Byrns as well. If we don't know what really happened in the war, then how can we understand the PTSD itself? In any situation, we should know all details, even the ones that are serious to truley understand a person's what they are going through. PTSD is serious. I've seen it affect my family & it's hard to watch. When we understand it, we understand the problem & person.

Figure 5.7

a Because the kids have never done a written conversation before, who knows how you address one a letter to a group?

b Jacob's article was a letter written by an American soldier in World War II, describing the carnage on the battlefield.

c This is not just pro forma agreement; both kids can elaborate reasons why they think public understanding of PTSD is so important.

Paper #2, started by Laveyn

> **LV!** As I was reading my article, I learned that PTSD not only affects the person who has it, but also their family and other close friends. The people around the person begin to wonder if they did something wrong or were the cause of unhappiness with the PTSD victim. It especially hard on children
>
> **LJ:** I agree 100% with you! PTSD is hard on the family as well as the victim. It brings more worry to the victim & the family. It just seems like a bad situation, but I personally believe that if the family is built around love, trust, & strength, they will make it through. ♡
>
> **Leyash.** I agree that if the family is built around love, they will make it through. Sometimes its extremely hard on the spouse because they feel the returned PTSD victim is not the same person they fell in love with because his/her complete attitude changed. They just have to know it will all get better with love and treatment.

Laveyn's article focused on the family impact of PTSD, and she reports a few specifics.

Lindsey strikes a very hopeful note, after adding some more details.

Leyash almost, but not quite, disagrees, wanting to emphasize how much there is to overcome with PTSD.

Figure 5.8

Paper #3, started by Lindsey

Lindsey

LC: Dear table,
When I read the WWII letter, I saw many signs of PTSD, including: guilt, scared, etc. But the main thing I saw was that he still loved & trusted his parents while writing this letter. He wanted them to see what was happening in this war. He wasn't ashamed to tell.

Leyash: Dear table,
Lindsey, he probably wanted his parents to know the truth so that when he returned they would know and understand why he was acting the way he did. He probably knew his parents had been there for him before, so he knew they would be there for him now and he probably wanted to let them know the truth

Jacob: Dear table,
You are both correct and Have really good Ideas. and I think though that He also needs the public to Know like He ssaid in the letter, I Know I would want everyone to Know, Bye

a Lindsey sets the subject of the shocked soldier's relationship with his parents, and Leyash and Jacob stick with it.

b Jacob adds the idea that the letter-writer probably wanted the world, not only his parents, to hear about the realities of war.

Figure 5.9

Paper #4, started by Ashley

Ashley / Ashley (Green)

Dear classmate,
  Because of the going and leaving so much, I believe that is a 'cause of PTSD. When people who have PTSD return, they are not the same. They do not want to do what they used to do. As a result, kids in military households often fear it is their fault, as do military spouses. They have to get treatment.

Jacob   I agree, some what, it May, be the reason, but I think there are More and definately worse reasons, such as the things they see, I agree it would be better for them to come Home more but when they do they Need somebody to be there!

  I agree with Byrns and LeyAsh. the constant leaving and coming back is tough on everyone, which supports what LeyAsh read. But the things that they see overseas and in battle are another big cause, which supports what Byrns read. We can ... agree or disagree on the biggest cause, but the Main part is that everyone with PTSD needs treatment.

Figure 5.10

a Having read an article about PTSD-affected soldiers coming home, Ashley speculates that the constant family separations of military service could be one cause of stress.

b Here, Jacob disagrees very agreeably. It's not just the separations, but the things soldiers see in war, that cause PTSD.

c Lindsey skillfully reviews and harmonizes both other kids' comments, asserting what they all agree on.

When we later shifted to whole-class discussion, several students came forward with stories, some harrowing, of the effects of PTSD on their own families. One reason for the frank and serious nature of the discussion, we'd argue, was that everyone had a chance to read and think and write about PTSD before they ever said anything aloud. The remarks people made were considered, grounded, and relevant.

After trying this kind of silent discussion for the first time, most of the kids were enthusiastic on the exit slips we asked them to fill out.

Written Convosations=
WIN.

I really liked all the activities, but My favorite was the one where we wrote notes. I enjoyed that one because you got to have a conversation silently while still getting your point across. I would really enjoy doing that in class. :)

The writing and passing it around was great!

My favorite thing we did today was writing the notes & mingling. It gave me a better chance to include my thoughts & combine them with others. I saw different sides of people & I understood the topics better.

I liked this whole experience because I'm a cronic thinker and it Makes you think what if you were in that situation? or what if you were around someone with PTSD? It Makes me go into deep thoughts + I will probably think about it all day now.

 Could we ask for a better outcome from any class activity?   Figure 5.11

Science

At Chicago's Disney II Magnet School, third-grade teacher Adrienne Garrison's kids are finishing up small-group inquiries on the sun and the moon, with subtopics including meteors, craters, volcanos, and "the light and dark side." Adrienne has encouraged kids to do their planning and reflecting in writing all the way through their investigations. Here, one team is putting the finishing touches on their upcoming report.

Dear Group,

I loved connecting our Qs and what we learned. It made me think about connections. Do they connect? What do you think we should tell the Flaming Surface group? I think we should go in # order, Alex, me, you, 6, 8, 10. I also think we should ask for feedback.

Tori

I actually agree with you because everything you said really made sence to me and because also that's a really good kind of example to start with. I think that I did really agree how you said we can go in number order. Also I think it was a great way how you said we should give feedback of how we all talked about the really good details of the sun.

Lujayn

Guys,

This project is a blast!!! Pretty cool, agree? Also I think we should come up with some more sticky notes for our sun poster. It may help connect questions & learning experience. But it will have to be deeper questions, agree? I love questions & doodles and teacher.

Alex

Yes it should be deeper Qs. It was fun working on the poster. You love doodles? Well we'll draw doodles of the sun if you want. Like I did in front of you but these would be color. We should decorate the name too, agree? I didn't like this project, I LOVED IT!!!!!

Tori

I liked when we were all talking about our connections of how we can kind of relate to and connect the dots.

Lujayn

We did relate with questions. Very smart article you did. I ☺ it and I ? it. We also needed smart brains like yours.

Alex

Alex said you have smart brains! You are smart and we definitely would not have been that interested if you weren't here. Alex you came up with great Qs!

Tori

You both are so kind to tell me that but you guys are the ones who are the smart ones and infact we all are the SMART ONES!!!

Lujayn

Gotta love that enthusiasm, plus, these 9-year-olds have a boatload of social skills. They are thinking, planning, piggybacking, negotiating, and supporting each other as learners all the way through the conversation.

WHAT COULD POSSIBLY GO WRONG?

Throughout this book, we've been showing you samples of successful written conversations between kids from all grade levels, and across the curriculum. And, truly, this peer-to-peer writing has a lot of allure for most students. But nothing *always* works. In one New Hampshire classroom, Smokey taught a U.S. Constitution lesson on freedom of religion. For a provocative text, he gave kids a short newspaper article about how Illinois students might be required to pray for one minute at the start of every school day. Figuring that this would rile up some interest among teenagers, he set kids up in write-around groups and turned them loose to discuss the constitutional issue. Most of the kids went right to the task, and the resulting whole-group discussion was energetic and thoughtful. But while collecting all the write-arounds later, it became painfully clear that one group of boys in the back hadn't been engaged at all.

SA: Dear Group, How about them Red Sox?

BT: Whoop whoop!

CT: I don't think it was a good law and it should be reviewed by the Supreme Court.

TD: Seriously this sux.

BT: Do you have gum?

SA: NONE

CT: It should go to the Supreme Court!

TD: Should go to the Supreme Court, have no gum, Red Sox won last night even though I don't follow baseball.

ALL: *scribbling in center of page*

Funny.

Red Sox Rule!!!

Hilarious.

Rockies Rule.

Cartoon Sam with a fro.

What's the moral of this story? Certainly not to give up on written conversations! For a better outcome next time, you could break up this particular group, or monitor the writing time more closely, or double-check kids' interest level before assuming you've got an engaging topic. But usually, the most powerful corrective, when any kind of lesson flops for some of the class, is to make it a mini lesson the next day:

> You guys, when I was reading through your write-arounds about the Second Amendment last night, I noticed that some groups stayed right on the topic, while some others got distracted and ended up just fooling around. So let's talk about that. What are some things that can make it hard to stay focused during a written conversation? Let's call these "off-task triggers," and we'll list some of them in the left column here. Then, on the other side of the page, we'll write down some possible solutions . . .

"Usually, the most powerful corrective, when any kind of lesson flops for some of the class, is to make it a mini lesson the next day."

Psychology

A few years back, we visited a high school classroom in Youngstown, Ohio, where teacher Roy Weingarten launched a lesson that ended in one of the liveliest write-arounds we've ever seen. Roy handed out a short excerpt about risk-taking among young people from Leonard Sax's 2005 book *Why Gender Matters*. It seems that investigators had devised a special video game that measured aggressiveness and danger-seeking by inviting players to go "over the limits," by crashing cars or swimming in a rip current, with potentially destructive consequences to their own avatars. Unsurprisingly, the results showed that boys were far more likely than girls to court danger in this game world.

Then, instead of inviting a whole-class discussion, Roy put the kids in write-around groups to discuss their reading. Because they had never done a written conversation before, he had to go through the instructions (on pages 168–169) step by step. But the novelty was attractive, and the kids dove into the writing. The teacher's last instructions were "What do you think of this research? Do you think this study's findings are correct, and true to life? Do boys take more risks than girls? If so, why is that?"

The written conversation among these six kids ranges over a wide array of responses, some superficial, some thoughtful, and many just killed us.

> **BG:** Why don't boys use their minds before they do something? They always have to prove that their better than someone else when they're really not. I wish they would just stop and think about what they do before they hurt themselves and others around them.

> **AMS:** I think that I agree because most boys just have to show off and don't think about what going to happen before its done and too late to correct. And they're not better than anybody—everybody's the same to me.

> **RMS:** I disagree with y'all. Boys show off but its only because girls provoke it. Come on now, girls aren't better than boys at some things?

We don't have the same abilities. Football and other physically oriented sports can't be played by girls. So you are right but you are wrong too. Yup!

AP: Write up, dude. I think boys are more risk takers than girls because girls are always worried about like their nails breaking or their hair messing up or their skin getting scarred.

BG: I think that goes both ways. Boys don't like messing up their clothes just like girls. Girls might be worried about their nails and hair, but boys be worried about their shoes and clothes and haircuts and their braids have to be fresh.

RMC: I know boys take more risks than girls because girls are more careful, but I think this test or game was dumb. Think about it: no boy I know is gonna want to get in a crash let alone be pumped up about it.

AP: Oh, yeah, that was dumb. Because I'm a boy and I don't enjoy getting into accidents or crashes because some crashes you might not live from and you can be hurt real bad.

SF: Yea, I agree with y'all because I know some boys who don't like getting hurt but they will keep doin' dangerous things and putting their self at risk. They must not care enough about it.

AMS: I think that boys take more risks because they don't care about what happens. They just have to prove their self and all. Girls they care about getting hurt and things like that and in some ways I think its bad but it's good cause it ain't me. Peace.

RMC: It ain't you and it sure as hell ain't me neither. I swear they only got white people taking this test. No offense but you know white people be all in with that dumb stuff. For real, though, who do you think wants to crash or swim in a strong beach current? That's adrenaline rushes white people have.

AP: Hell yeah. Whites are the only people who get a rush from hurting themselves. No disrespect to white people. I love white people.

There were no white people in the room to be offended, except us, but we were too busy laughing about our trail-biking/hang-gliding/rock-climbing friends and their "adrenaline rushes" back in New Mexico.

TEXT ON TEXT

You might call text on text "right-brain write-arounds." Instead of a nice orderly passing of separate notes from one person to the next, this is more of a happy free-for-all. Everybody writes on the same big piece of chart paper, which has a prompt or short piece of text (fiction or nonfiction, or an image or photo) pasted in the center. Many teachers like to use a puzzling or controversial text to stir different responses and contradictory interpretations. The idea is to provoke an extended conversation in the margins, as kids gradually study, respond to, comment on, challenge, and even dispute what their buddies have written.

This unique letter variation begins with text annotation, the practice whereby savvy readers mark up texts with marginal notes, underlinings, highlights, and/or codes (we explored this on pages 160–161). This kind of marking leaves visible tracks of the reader's thinking, and reminds us that proficient readers don't magically zoom though print, but actually stop, think, and react as they go. And the most important part of annotation is jotting words in the margins—words that remind you later what you thought, wondered, disputed, or learned.

"This kind of marking reminds us that proficient readers don't magically zoom though print, but actually stop, think, and react as they go."

So, text on text is what happens when you have *several* kids annotate the same copy of a text at the same time, jotting their responses in the margins. Quite naturally, students start reading other people's comments and want to give their classmates a written high five, ask a clarifying question, or throw down a tough challenge. Just like a regular write-around, this is a silent activity, but that doesn't mean it's docile. Since everyone is writing on the same page at once, kids sometimes run into each other's hands while writing, and have to go over, under, around, or though. This sounds a little out of control, but when kids are really building upon each other's interpretations, it's more energetic and competitive than crazy.

Smokey: A couple of years back, I was working in a very poor rural school district. As I got to know the friendly and eager kids, I recognized that they were quite unused to small-group discussions, whether out-loud or in writing. So, in one history class, I handed out a short nonfiction article and, using my handy-dandy portable document camera, modeled how to annotate the text, using simple codes and marginal notes. But when I asked them to try it, not a single kid would put one annotation on the handout in front of them. The kids weren't being defiant, but they silently refused to annotate.

I must have looked pretty puzzled because the classroom teacher walked up and whispered to me, "We never allow kids to mark on a handout. We can't afford to copy more than one class set, so we have to reuse them for all five classes. Usually, they'd get in trouble if they mark up those copies." Whew. Talk about the unseen costs of underfunded schools. He also confided to me that the kids really hated writing and didn't do it very much in school. Perfect! So lack of annotation practice plus writing phobia. Time for text on text.

For the next class, I grabbed a pad of big chart paper and some markers out of my car and got special permission to make nine copies of a great Gary Soto poem, "Mission Tire Factory, 1969." This is a most teen-friendly poem about a factory worker who gets his arm severed in a horrific machine accident, and then gives his buddies money for lunch as he is being wheeled to the ambulance. Powerful stuff.

I stuck the copies of the poem in the center of each piece of poster paper. Then I went off to the classroom and pushed desks together so that there would be three kids, each with a different color pen, sitting around each "poem chart." When the kids came in, I told them what we were up to. They still seemed hesitant about writing on this jumbo-sized handout, so I added one more instruction: "Feel free to *draw* your reaction to the poem—you don't have to write words." Just as we discussed earlier, drawing can be the bridge into writing for many kids. Finally, I read the poem aloud to get them started and then floated from group to group as they very slowly began putting a few marks down on their charts. See Figure 5.13 for one example.

After some writing and drawing time, I told kids that they could talk out loud, and the classroom burst into lively conversation about Soto and the poem.

With more practice and instruction, this kind of collaborative annotation can go much deeper. In Kennett High School in North Conway, New Hampshire, teacher Carrie Costello used text on text to support a student discussion of a section of Walt Whitman's "Leaves of Grass." Six students (too many for us!) jammed themselves around this page and, each in their own color pen, contributed to the following discussion.

With all the arrows and lines, it's a little hard to follow the strands of conversation. So we've transcribed them on page 189 to show the three main conversations that developed, using the kids' pen colors to identify each writer. In the first strand, students are primarily fact-checking what the poet says.

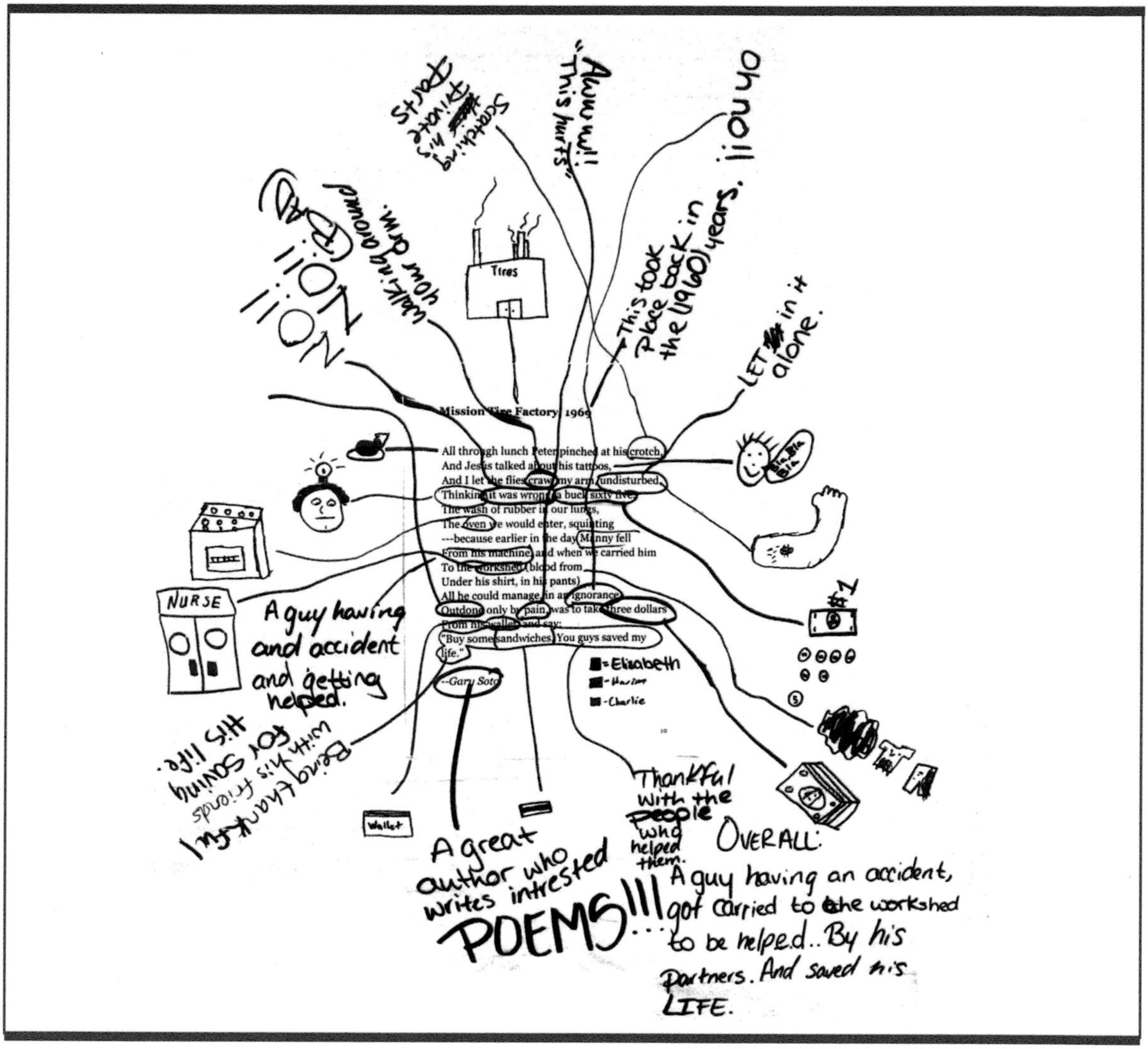

For the student with the red pen, drawing and cartooning were the preferred mode of response.

The other two kids used a mixture of drawing and writing.

All three were working mostly at the factual level, trying to clarify their understanding of the poem. And yet you can feel the energy emerging on the page.

Source: Gary Soto: New and Selected Poems © by Gary Soto Used with permission of Chronicle Books LLC, San Francisco. Visit ChornicleBooks.com.

Figure 5.13

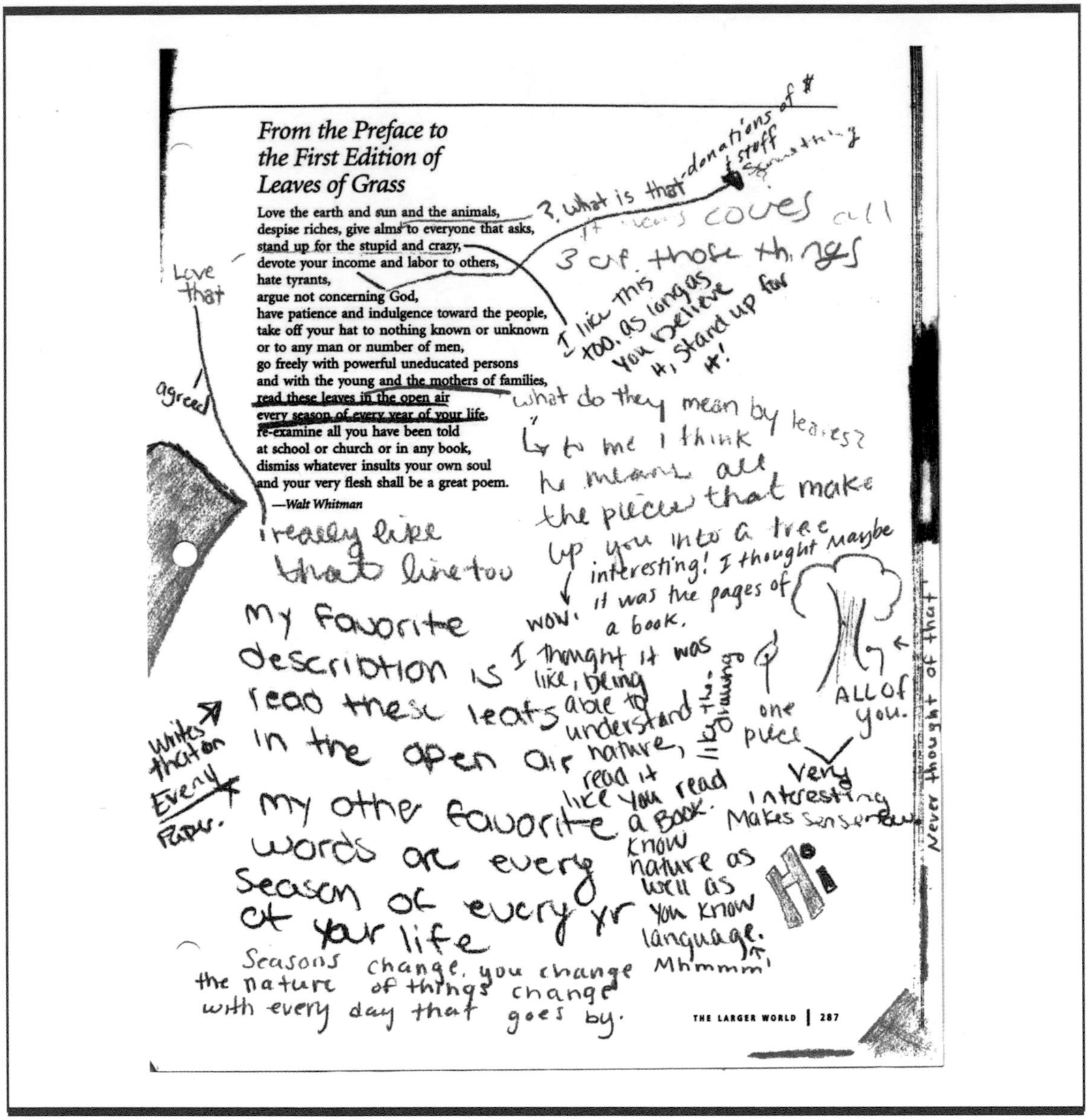

From the Preface to the First Edition of Leaves of Grass

Love the earth and sun and the animals,
despise riches, give alms to everyone that asks,
stand up for the stupid and crazy,
devote your income and labor to others,
hate tyrants,
argue not concerning God,
have patience and indulgence toward the people,
take off your hat to nothing known or unknown
or to any man or number of men,
go freely with powerful uneducated persons
and with the young and the mothers of families,
read these leaves in the open air
every season of every year of your life,
re-examine all you have been told
at school or church or in any book,
dismiss whatever insults your own soul
and your very flesh shall be a great poem.

—Walt Whitman

Handwritten annotations:

Love that

agreed

? what is that donations of $ stuff something

It was covers all 3 of those things

I like this too. as long as you believe for it, stand up for it!

what do they mean by leaves? to me I think he means all the pieces that make up you into a tree interesting! I thought maybe it was the pages of a book.

i really like that line too

My favorite description is read these leats in the open air

wow! I thought it was like, being able to understand the nature, read it like you read a book. know nature as well as you know language.

one piece

ALL of you.

Very Interesting Makes sense too

Never thought of that

my other favorite words are every season of every yr of your life

Writes that for Every paper.

Seasons change, you change, the nature of things change with every day that goes by.

Mhmmm!

THE LARGER WORLD | 287

We get a good sense of the kids' engagement level just by looking at the page.
They're obviously digging into the poem and connecting with each other's' thinking.
For more detail, see page 189.

Figure 5.14

Red: ? what is that ("give alms")

Gray: Donations of $ and stuff

Brown: Something . . .

Blue: the poet loves all three of those things ("the earth, the sun, and the animals")

Next, kids focus on one prominent line.

Red: Love that ("stand up for the stupid and crazy")

Gray: I like this too, as long as you believe it, stand up for it!

Brown: agreed

Green: I really like that line too

Now they dig deeper into the imagery of the poem.

Red: What do they mean by leaves?

Green: To me I think he means all the pieces that make up you like a tree.

Gray: Interesting! I thought it was maybe pages of a book.

Green: *Draws picture of a leaf labeled* "one piece" *and a tree labeled* "all of you."

Brown: Like the drawing. Very interesting, makes sense now.

Red: Never thought of that!

Gray: Wow. I thought it was like being able to understand nature, read it like you read a book. Know nature as well as you know language.

Red: Mhmmm!

Orange: My favorite description is read these leafs in the open air. My other favorite words are every season of every year of your life.

Red: Seasons change, you change, the nature of things changes with every day that goes by.

Here we see once again the phenomenon where students' thinking deepens through written conversation: As the kids get further into the poem, they move from literal to inferential and interpretive talk about Whitman's message.

MANAGEMENT TIPS FOR WRITE-AROUNDS

Group Size. The optimum size for write-arounds is three or four. This provides the right balance of positive social pressure with just enough diversity to make the discussion interesting. One valuable wrinkle is that you can have kids sitting in groups of four or five, but only have them write and pass three times. That way, every single member is joining in the topic, but won't see everyone else's notes—nor does he or she need to. This mechanism helps us to resolve uneven classroom numbers as we form write-around groups; if threes don't come out even, we can have a couple groups of four and not worry about it. Still, we ideally like to match the number of kids in each group to the number of letters we expect them to write and pass.

Group Formation. When doing this for the first time, it's a good idea to either form the groups yourself or use a random grouping generator (there are many free choices online). Early in the year, we want kids to work with different classmates every day; this helps build acquaintance and support in the classroom. When wide friendship is established, you can let kids pick their own writing pals as long as they keep changing around periodcally. Later in the year, students can *apply to you* to propose an ongoing write-around group. They must explain why these particular three or four students would work well together.

Length of Writing Time for Each Letter. This can range from a half-minute to several minutes, depending on the lesson purpose. We have a colleague who has kids do one-sentence write-arounds and then leave them as an exit slip at the end of math class—and others who have kids write for five solid minutes per letter. Of course, if students are writing by hand, there are physical limits. Hands just get tired, especially since we are all now keyboarders, hopelessly out of shape for handwriting, even if we learned it in the first place. Average writing time: one and a half to three minutes.

Passing Papers. It can become a comical fire drill if you simply tell kids, "Pass your papers" or even "Pass your paper to someone else." "Clockwise" doesn't work either, because so many people have to sit there and figure out which way a clock goes and then convert it to a horizontal plane. Have kids sit in their group first, and establish which way passes will go before the writing starts. "Left" or "right" works fine.

Number of Exchanges. There is something almost spooky about this: Two changes isn't enough to get much of a conversation going, three notes is often good, four is sometimes much better than three, and five is almost always too many. Weird, huh? Now, that's for live write-arounds; when we shift to the digital version, where kids are posting to online discussions, you may well have 30 or 60 posts in a string. But in typical whole-class online discussions, each kid will probably only put in one to three contributions, so the degree of individual participation may be similar to the old-school, small-group live version. Much more on this in Chapter 6.

Reluctant/Slow/Struggling Writers. First of all, drawing must be legalized as a perfectly satisfactory way to take part in written discussion; that gives a lot of kids the opening they need to get started. Then you can group kids by their speed of text production so that everyone who's working together gets about the same amount of writing down in a given amount of time. We also sometimes "lie" about the timing; we will tell kids, "Just write for a minute," but actually wait until everyone has some writing done before calling for paper passes.

Shifting to Out-Loud Discussion. After a few passes, we often want write-around groups to put down their pens and continue the conversation out loud. Sometimes kids can make this jump from writing to talk without any guidance from us. Other times, there can be a lag. So, to be sure this transition happens smoothly, we always have a very specific prompt ready to get kids talking. "Now read over the page you are holding and circle the one most interesting or puzzling sentence that anyone wrote. To start the out-loud discussion, have someone read his or her circled sentence aloud."

Quotas. Just as with nondigital letters, we will sometimes have kids who need concrete targets, goals, or quotas in order to sustain an effort. We can express these as a minimum number of lines or paragraphs written, a number of posts per session, or this much time on a task. We prefer to negotiate these standards with kids rather than just announce them. ("OK, guys, what would be a reasonable number of posts to show that you are really into this kind of discussion?") In any case, it's not OK to not join in. Kids who are seeking a zero should not be denied one.

CHAPTER 6

Digital Discussions

Dear Reader,

Do your kids' wrists get tired from handwriting letters to their classmates? No worries—almost every type of written conversation we have talked about so far has a digital equivalent. And then there are a host of other discussions that you can only have digitally. Check it out.

Smokey and Elaine

DEFINITION: Digital discussions are written conversations we can have using the amazing tech tools of our age: email, blogs, wikis, message boards, texting, and all the rest. Sometimes these devices and channels allow us to work more quickly, instantly add illustrations or attachments, and include much wider audiences than we can with paper and pencil. And yet, for the most part, what we actually say or write to each other is mostly the same: We connect, share, play, discuss, comment, challenge, debate, advise, and compromise.

VARIATIONS:

- Texted Discussions
- Photo Journals
- Lab Letters
- Blogs
- Online Partnerships
- Email and Farewell

ORIGINS: Obviously our contemporary conversational hardware, software, and apps derive from old analog tools—or from earlier computer-based utilities. We've had telephones forever, email for 20 years, and texting for what, 10 minutes? What's really fun is exploring the dazzling array of new kid-friendly programs coming out almost daily: Kidblog, SonicPics, Songify, Google Hangouts, TodaysMeet, and others. The history of professional books on teaching with new technology is, not surprisingly, short and narrow. We think the best tech book for secondary teachers is *Adolescents and Digital Literacies: Learning Alongside Our Students* by Sara Kajder (2010). And a wonderful tech resource for elementary teachers—*Connecting Comprehension and Technology*—has just been released by our colleagues Stephanie Harvey, Anne Goudvis, Kristin Ziemke, and Katie Muhtaris (2013).

QUICK LOOK:

Texted Discussions

At Springfield High School, the social studies curriculum calls for a four-week unit on westward expansion. This morning, U.S. history teacher Joe Occipinti has been introducing the idea of Manifest Destiny by showing a painting by

John Gast called *American Progress*. This picture shows a beautiful female figure in a slightly incongruous low-cut white gown, floating over the Midwestern United States, circa 1845. Underneath her, westward expansion is happening in every corner of the image, moving from right to left. Settlers, farmers, ranchers, and miners stream from the east on foot, in wagons, and on railroads—while Indians and large animals flee toward the Rockies.

Seated beside each other in the second row, Steven and Madeleine are "writing break" partners. Some days, prearranged pairs of Joe's students take out index cards and have brief written conversations when he pauses his lecture a few times per period (see pages 89–91). During these quickwrites, kids clarify their developing understanding and raise any questions that need attention before Joe goes on. Today, they're having such a conversation, but instead of writing on paper, they are *texting on their own cell phones*. Unlike most of the surrounding districts, Springfield encourages the use of kids' phones in classes. So when Joe invites kids to enjoy a midclass writing break, they can do it digitally.

Steven: Whoa, her dress is totally falling off. ☺

    Madeleine: Get your mind off her wardrobe, you perv!

Steven: Just saying . . .

    Madeleine: So who is this lady/person? White gown . . .

Steven: Like some kind of angel, coming down to earth.

    Madeleine: This has to be America in the 1840s.

Steven: Why else would Mr O be showing us this??

Steven: So what city is that on the right side? Harbor, etc?

    Madeleine: Must be NY, maybe Boston? The east, it is east on the country.

Steven: So she is hovering over, like Ohio, Kentucky?

Madeleine: See the people under her . . . like farmers, and wagon guys

Steven: And miners, one guy has an pick-ax

Madeleine: Oh, they're all moving west, get it!?

Steven: Duh.

SEND

They look up at each other and laugh aloud. Back to the phones.

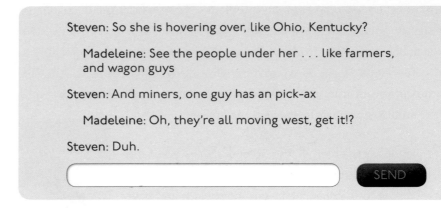

Madeleine: See how the whole picture gets darker as you look west?

Steven: Where the Indians are running away, and the buffaloes.

Madeleine: Why would it be darker?

Steven: Maybe b/c its scary and unknown area. After the rocky mts nobody knew what was out there.

Madeleine: Is that a Bible she is carrying?

Steven: Probably—I just noticed that she is stringing those wires through her hands, phone wires . . .

Madeleine: Probably telegraph, it's like 1845.

Steven: Right, yeah.

SEND

Texting appears to violate one of the rules of written conversations: that partners always write simultaneously on separate pieces of paper. When you are texting, you are essentially creating one written conversation, not two. You take turns, waiting while your partner writes. Normally, we don't want kids just watching someone else write. But in the actual practice of texting, we write so quickly and respond so often that there really isn't much waiting—and, of course, we often start writing our next text before we even see what our partner is writing to us.

The teacher announces, "One more minute. What's the overall gist of the picture?"

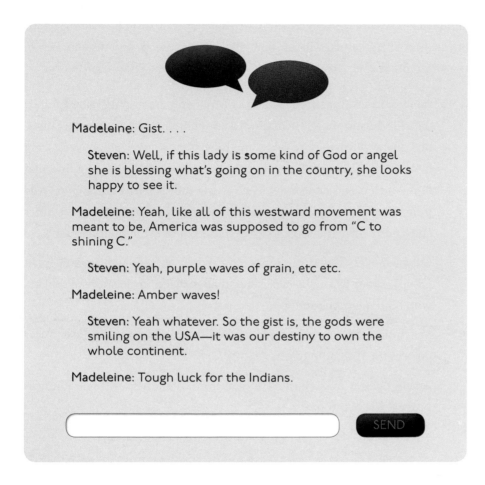

Madeleine: Gist. . . .

Steven: Well, if this lady is some kind of God or angel she is blessing what's going on in the country, she looks happy to see it.

Madeleine: Yeah, like all of this westward movement was meant to be, America was supposed to go from "C to shining C."

Steven: Yeah, purple waves of grain, etc etc.

Madeleine: Amber waves!

Steven: Yeah whatever. So the gist is, the gods were smiling on the USA—it was our destiny to own the whole continent.

Madeleine: Tough luck for the Indians.

SEND

Now this kind of texted discussion isn't exactly the same as its written version. Comments are naturally shorter and are exchanged more frequently. The temptation to look up and talk instead is strong—and what's wrong with that? A little chatter enlivens the experience, as long as we've trained kids to use texting as the baseline.

LAUNCHING LESSON:

Photo Journals

In her first-grade classroom in Chicago, Kristin Ziemke blends traditional paper-and-pencil activities with high-tech tools. Today the kids will be reading a variety of short science articles about topics like plants, insects, and the sun. Before they head off to read, Kristin gathers kids on the rug for a short chart lesson.

"Smart readers stop, think, and react while they are reading," she reminds the kids. Kristin shows them how to annotate their texts with a big question mark when they notice something they wonder about, and a big L for "new learning" whenever they discover some interesting information. She lets kids choose a science article they *can read* and *want to read* from among several choices, and then kids head off with Post-it notes and skinny markers. "Go and leave tracks of your thinking," she advises.

Kristin moves around the room, conferring with individuals and small groups as they work. She makes sure that everyone creates several stickies, with both questions and some new learnings.

Marco has written a pretty good question about his insect article: "How do bees use the bathroom?"

Kristin doesn't miss a beat. "Do you think the article will tell you how bees use the bathroom?"

Marco nods. "Maybe they go inside the leaves and hide there."

"Well, using the bathroom is something that all humans and animals do. Why don't you put a question-mark Post-it there and keep reading?"

Circulating around the room once more, Kristin tells the kids, "Bring it back everybody." When kids are gathered on the rug, she explains the next step.

"Here's what I want you to do next. In just a minute, I'm going to send you back to your tables, and you're going to take a photo of one of your Post-its, open SonicPics, upload it, and do a short recording. I'd love to hear one piece of new learning and one question from your reading and work today. So, you're going to get your iPad, take a photo, go to SonicPics, and do a little video recording. Questions? Yes?"

Tess wonders, "Do you want the questions and new learning separate?"

"You can do them all in the same podcast. So I will get a good selection of them and I can go and listen at home, because I didn't have a chance to check in with everybody to see what your new learning and all your great questions were. So if you make a little podcast, then I'll be able to see what you're working on, and I'll be able to plan for more learning over the next couple of days. So show me your best Post-its!"

At a table near the window, Marissa pulls out her iPad and snaps a photo of her favorite new learning Post-it.

Figure 6.1

Then she dictates into SonicPics: "I learned that the sun is a hot ball of glowing gasses. It also is the center of our solar system. And that's what I learned." She closes the program and emails her podcast to Ms. Ziemke. A few hours later in her kitchen, Kristin will open Marissa's email and enjoy her thinking. She'll think about what Marissa and all the other kids have shared, and go back to class tomorrow, ready to take the just-right next steps with her young readers.

LAB LETTERS

Purpose: In some schools, in order to have digital written conversations, we have to visit the computer lab.

Of course, not all schools have iPads for every kid quite yet. In a more typical classroom in suburban Chicago, the only web space kids can use is when they march down to the computer lab and post on a common page. No problem, says English teacher Danielle Schwartz, and off her kids go to have a digital discussion of Walter Dean Myers's wonderful young adult novel *Monster*. In this gripping story, likable 16-year-old Steve Harmon, an African American kid in Chicago, gets tangentially involved in a planned holdup. Then it all goes wrong, someone gets shot, and he finds himself on trial for murder, as an accomplice to a felony. Within the first few pages of the book, the prosecutor points his finger at Steve and tells the jury, "Ladies and gentleman, this is a monster!"

As her students sit down at their individual computers, Danielle wants to be sure they have a focused conversation on pages 1 through 43 of the book. So she types this prompt for everyone to see as they log on.

> Why do you think Walter Dean Myers chose to write this novel in the form of a screenplay instead of normal narrative prose? Post your thoughts on this question, listen to everyone, and keep the conversation going.

Here's what several students chipped in:

> **Re: Re: Monster Reading** . . . pages 1–43
> by student132 at 12:15PM (CDT) on Oct 16
>
> I think he chose to write a screenplay because it seems like something that would be on TV. And yes I've felt like my life is a movie before many, many times. Mainly when I have a really good day or a really bad day.

> REPLY
>
> **Re: Re: Monster Reading** . . . pages 1–43
> by student141 at 10:03PM (CDT) on Oct 18
>
> > Totally agreeing with you, many many many times I've thought of my life like a movie (or Tv show or etc.) but I think he chose to write his story as a screenplay because it made it seem more real, well more interesting and how it actually happened.
>
> REPLY
>
> **Re: Re: Monster Reading** . . . pages 1–43
> by student117 at 5:21PM (CDT) on Oct 18
>
> > I think the reason that the author chose a screen play format is that it will help us to visualize the story more and get "that movie in our head" going so we will understand better what it is like to be in certain characters shoes.
>
> REPLY
>
> **Re: Re: Monster Reading** . . . pages 1–43
> by student109 at 5:22PM (CDT) on Oct 18
>
> > Right in the book it says how Steve feels like he is trapped in some terrible movie about him. Like it cant really be happening but it is.I kinda like all this zoom in and fade to black stuff, it makes you feel like it IS a movie your watching.

Notice the gradually deepening focus on the assigned topic. We often see this dynamic in written conversations. The first commenters may offer simple personal connections (my life is like a movie, we all have bad days, etc.). But the longer the discussion goes on, the better kids tend to address the topic and comment thoughtfully.

Figure 6.2

BLOGS

Purpose: Posting and responding on the web opens countless possibilities for kids to enter into discussions with others, near and far.

Management

Once you have created a classroom web space—whether you're using a site like Edmodo or a space provided by your district—you've just acquired a fantastic management tool. In a minute, we'll get to the academic discussions that this venue potentiates. But first, let's point out that having a common meeting place provides a natural venue for class news, assignments, schedules, handouts, questions and answers, and all manner of virtual fist-bumps.

In her classroom in Chicago (and now in California), middle school teacher Sara Ahmed uses an Edmodo page as the digital headquarters for most classroom business. In Chapter 1, we shared a long string of her students' comments about the causes of the Cold War (pages 13–15). What we didn't point out there is how her class website provides all the management support needed to help such thoughtful student interactions happen.

The Cold War conversation began when Sara posted two handouts right on the Edmodo page for kids to grab. She also spelled out the reading assignment and gave a prompt for the online discussion:

> SKAHMED: Here are excerpts from two articles about the origins of the Cold War. After you read them, everyone post at least once tonight. What did you learn, how do their points of view connect or conflict, what surprised you, and what questions do you have? Read what other people are posting and get a good conversation going. We'll start tomorrow by talking about this!

Kids can go to the class blog page anytime to review instructions, find materials, check in with the teacher, or make plans with classmates.

In Brenda George's class, students frequently use their classroom blog just to conduct simple business with each other:

> JREINER: Hey, did anyone pick up that Discover magazine with Lincoln on the cover?

> BENA: Nope, sorry.

> JROHAN: We were using it in our group, left it on the cable table.

> JREINER: Thx. I'll get it tomorrow.

And students can always communicate with the teacher.

> CINDYF: Ms G, is it too late for me to change my research topic from Eisenhower's speech to Faubus's speech?

> BGEORGE: I think you have plenty of time, no worries. Do you mean Faubus' speech opposing LRCHS integration? There's another one a year later when they closed the school system to avoid another year of integration. It's pretty amazing.

> CINDYF: yes! I'd like to read #2 speech.

> BGEORGE: I'll give you a copy tomorrow or Google it using "Faubus speech 1958."

> CINDYF: Thanks!

And (as we always prefer) the kids can do their own self-management online. Here, some kids in Natalie Fitterman's class on Long Island use the class blog to put together a "literature circle" book club—choosing a book, gathering a team, assigning everyone a reading role, scheduling their reading, and beginning to think about a beyond-the-book project.

What book r we reading next?

We finished the book Ms. Fitterman gave us, now we gotta start another, we all gotta pick a single book, and a group book. So someone's gotta do it.

Posted by K-dawg 4:45 PM

Dude I'm In

The blog is amazing . . . let's start reading!! Ha ha yeah right

Posted by Joe M 5:06 PM

We figured out what book we're readin

We're reading Holes, and we're watching the movie and comparing it to the movie, so everybody get the book, ight.

Posted by K-dawg 5:09 PM

Guys I'm in too.

Eddie B is in the house we gunna rock this book "Holes." YEAH YEAH!

Posted by Eddie B 7:53 PM

Project Jobs:

Kristian M—Word Wizard I

Joe M—project coordinator

Joe C—Essence Illustrator

Eddy B—Quotable quoter

Ali F—Lit Critic

Devin F—Word Wizard II

Posted by Ali F 7:59 PM

I just got in

I finally got in so I guess we have to start reading the book soon. First everyone in the group needs to get their book. It would help if we made a schedule of what pages we have to read every night so we aren't behind. I'm going to assume that's the project coordinator's job . . . my job for this part of the book is lit critic and we will have to hand in our role sheets by Thursday

Posted by Ali F 9:04 PM

Watch what the cynic chips in a few posts from now.   Figure 6.3 (continued)

Figure 6.3 (continued)

▶ **b**

Decision

Our group has made an executive choice for our book Holes.

As a group we have decided to read approximately 5 chapters a night. Considering that there is 50 chapters in the book, we will finish the book is about 10 days or maybe less because we are reading in class too. Overall this will leave us 5 days to finish our essay.

We have also decided to make an alternate ending to the book and movie. But we have not decided what part of the move to start from or what chapter.

Posted by Joe M 7:45 AM

A week later . . .

▶ **c**

HOLES THE ALTERNATE ENDING

I started the intro to our movie. Itz awesome/itz got the song BEAT IT and the roles for the movie are, Ali is gonna be da warden and Kissing Kate Barlow, I'm the camera man and any other peoplez we need. Eddy is all of the bunk members at Camp Greenlake, Joe M is Stanley Yelnats and Dr. Pandganski, Devin F as Mr. Sir and other peoplez. And Joe C as zero. Itz really kewl, we can start the move on Saturday

Posted by K-dawg 5:02 PM

▶ **b** Notice that this engaged note comes from Mr. "Ha ha yeah right."   Figure 6.3

▶ **c** Because the kids know that Ms. Fitterman is reading everything they blog, this serves as an official report to her that they have chosen their book and made a reading calendar.

Blog Discussions

Purpose: An efficient way for many kids—or all kids—to compose and post responses to classroom topics.

When we have written conversations online, we usually just call it blogging. Kids can meet up to chat about the stories they've read, the events they are studying, the projects they are completing, and the ideas the teachers are teaching. Indeed, the very existence of classroom blogs is reminding teachers how useful and motivating student-to-student correspondence can be. But kids aren't born knowing how to post on a blog; we have to teach them the rules of the digital road.

Back in Kristin Ziemke's first-grade classroom, we can see how she prepares kids for digital discussions. In a minute, Kristin's lucky 6-year-olds will be jumping on their individual iPads (insert envious sigh here). But first, using some distinctly low-tech chart paper and markers, Kristin asks her students to suggest some ways that people can have really fun and interesting digital discussions. The kids eagerly toss out ideas, and Kristin jots them on a "looks like/sounds like" T-chart.

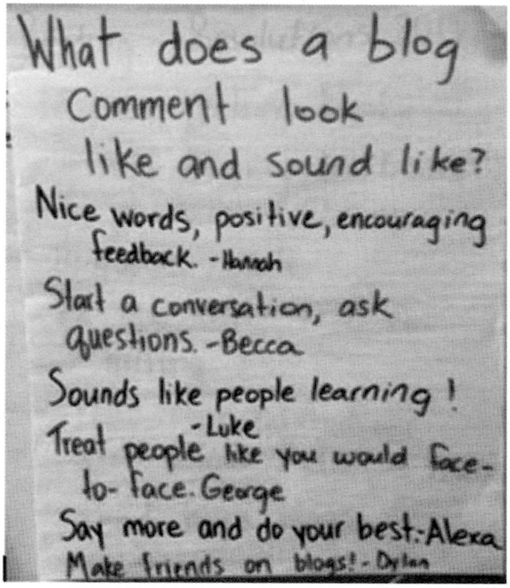

Looking over these suggestions from 6-year-olds, we see some pretty savvy thinking; in fact, this list would work pretty well for middle or high school kids as well.

Figure 6.4

Upstairs, in Michelle Nash's fifth-grade classroom at the same school, the kids are reading this week's issue of *Time for Kids* magazine, a great source of nonfiction text for intermediate-grade readers. Uma has chosen an article about Ada Lovelace, an unsung pioneer of the computer age, and is sharing her reading notes and a response about the piece.

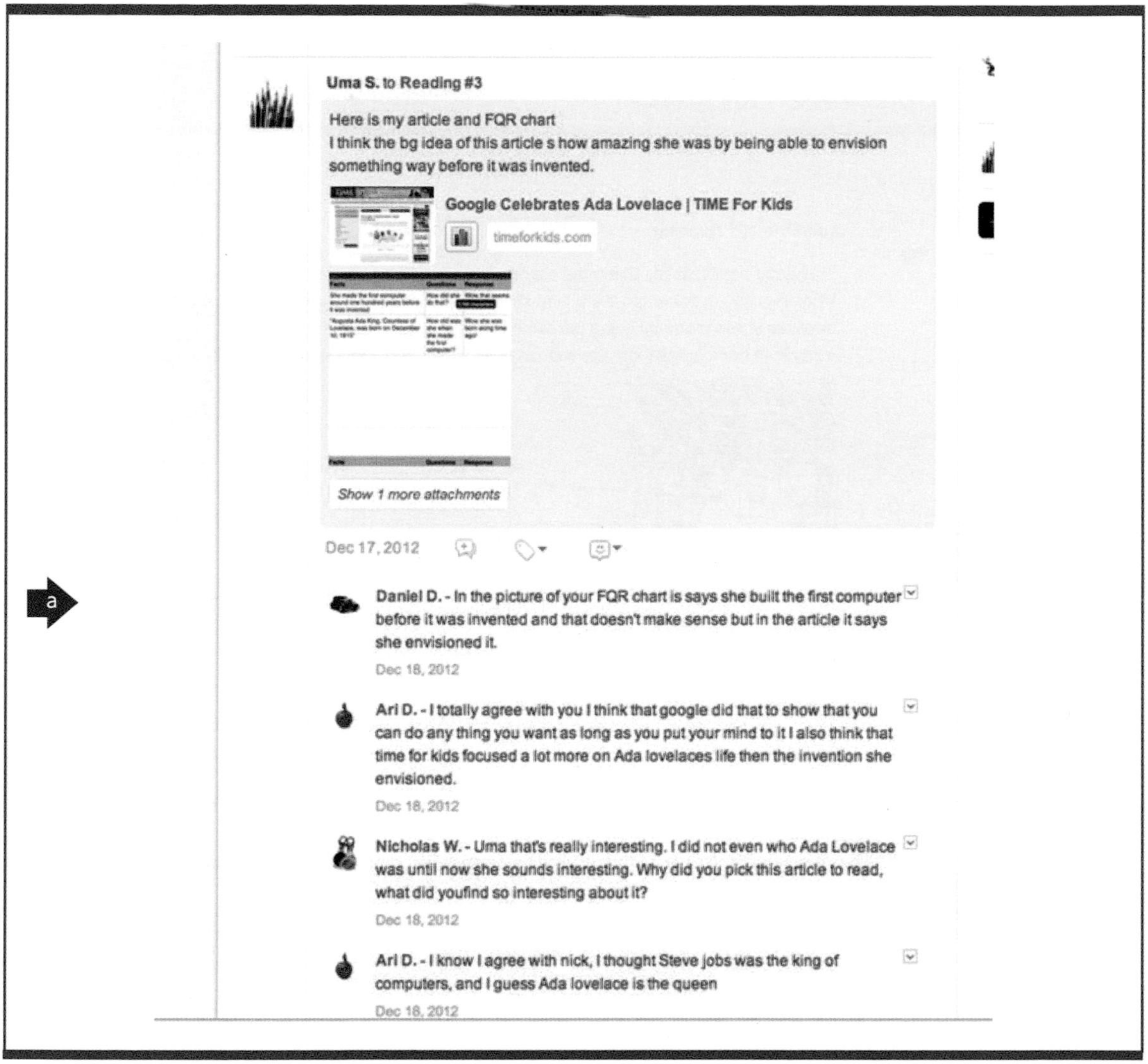

Uma S. to Reading #3

Here is my article and FQR chart
I think the bg idea of this article s how amazing she was by being able to envision something way before it was invented.

Google Celebrates Ada Lovelace | TIME For Kids
timeforkids.com

Show 1 more attachments

Dec 17, 2012

> **Daniel D.** - In the picture of your FQR chart is says she built the first computer before it was invented and that doesn't make sense but in the article it says she envisioned it.
> Dec 18, 2012

> **Ari D.** - I totally agree with you I think that google did that to show that you can do any thing you want as long as you put your mind to it I also think that time for kids focused a lot more on Ada lovelaces life then the invention she envisioned.
> Dec 18, 2012

> **Nicholas W.** - Uma that's really interesting. I did not even who Ada Lovelace was until now she sounds interesting. Why did you pick this article to read, what did you find so interesting about it?
> Dec 18, 2012

> **Ari D.** - I know I agree with nick, I thought Steve jobs was the king of computers, and I guess Ada lovelace is the queen
> Dec 18, 2012

(a) Notice the language that shows kids are really listening and responding to each other: "I totally agree with you"; "Uma that's really interesting"; "I know I agree with nick." Some teachers officially encourage kids to use each other's names in these dialogues as way of explicitly thinking about their audience.

Figure 6.5

As kids chose and read different chosen articles, Michelle asked them to do a form of note-taking called FQR, which stands for facts, questions, and responses, developed by Stephanie Harvey and Anne Goudvis (2007). While they read, kids stop and chart important information as they go. When it's time to share, kids post their chart as well as a written response, so students who haven't read the same piece will be informed enough to respond—and maybe motivated to read the article themselves.

Figure 6.6

When kids have digital discussions, they can also augment—or simply conduct—the conversation with drawings, sketches, maps, diagrams, stick figure scenes, or cartoons. We argued earlier that drawing is a vital letter-writing tool for all primary kids, as well as many language learners and kids with special needs—and, come to think of it, everyone. That's true for online conversations too, from little drop-in emoticons to full-fledged, handmade illustrations.

So, in Michelle's class, Lulu supplemented her reading blog with this lovely drawing, and got a thoughtful comment from Ari (see Figure 6.6).

In their seventh-grade history class, Sara Ahmed's students are studying the terrible Triangle Shirtwaist factory fire of 1923, in which 146 mostly young female sweatshop workers were killed. While there is still uncertainty about what actually sparked the blaze, multiple factors contributed to the horrific death toll. To get kids digging deeper into their readings about the event, Sara offers the discussion topic shown in Figure 6.6—and coaches the discussion closely.

The conversation in Figure 6.7 is very much of the sort envisioned by the Common Core State Standards for writing. Kids are required to read a set of complex nonfiction texts, make comparisons and contrast within the readings, take a position based on information in the text, and then develop well-supported argumentative texts in response. And this online discussion format has the advantage of being sociable and engaging.

"When kids have digital discussions, they can also augment—or simply conduct—the conversation with drawings, sketches, maps, diagrams, stick figure scenes, or cartoons."

"The conversation in Figure 6.7 is very much of the sort envisioned by the Common Core State Standards for writing."

Me to Ahmed7 Period 5

11/29 DISCUSSION QUESTION: What caused the Triangle Shirtwaist Fire Tragedy? Be careful, this is not a simple answer. Use evidence in your responses and push each other's thinking. I am looking for thoughtful responses, not the amount of responses.

Nov 29, 2012

Iberia (Ibi) V. - This is a tough topic to bring up considering most websites don't have an explanation for the cause of the fire. I believe that the dreadful flames may have started from a lit match simply being misplaced. Perhaps near oilcans? There was even a report of picked up cigarettes near the spot of the fires beginnings. Any thoughts? Oh and by the way, I got this information from this website: http://law2.umkc.edu/faculty/projects/ftrials...
Nov 29, 2012

Layne F. - In the New York times article it states, "flames suddenly leaped from a wastebasket under a table in the cutters' area." Maybe there was a cigarette like Ibi said, or a match could have been there also. Those two things could have definitely been inside a trashcan and could have started a fire if the flame was not distinguished properly. I don't think someone would have started it on purpose, or perhaps a citizen of the US started the fire. The New York times article says that immigrants worked in the company. Maybe the citizen did not like immigrants and wanted them all to die out. This may be an unreasonable guess, but I do find it kind of strange how the fire came out of nowhere. *less...*
Nov 29, 2012

Kiara J. - We will NEVER what REALLY caused the Triangle Shirtwaist Fire Tragedy. Reports state a cutter noticed a small fire had started in his waste bin. This fire was believed to have started by a match or a lit cigarette. Nearly everything in the room was flammable. Many pounds of cotton scraps, tissue paper and wooden tables; anyone in that place was destined for death.

The kids are making text-based responses here, searching for evidence in their research materials and then trying to draw reasonable inferences from it.

Figure 6.7 (continued)

Figure 6.7 (continued)

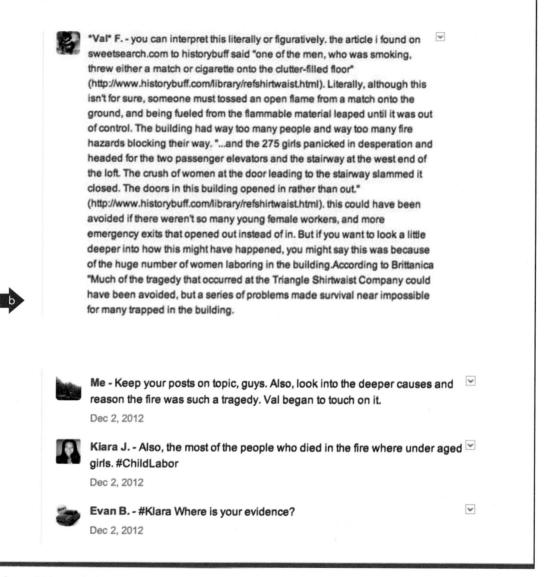

Val F. - you can interpret this literally or figuratively. the article i found on sweetsearch.com to historybuff said "one of the men, who was smoking, threw either a match or cigarette onto the clutter-filled floor" (http://www.historybuff.com/library/refshirtwaist.html). Literally, although this isn't for sure, someone must tossed an open flame from a match onto the ground, and being fueled from the flammable material leaped until it was out of control. The building had way too many people and way too many fire hazards blocking their way. "...and the 275 girls panicked in desperation and headed for the two passenger elevators and the stairway at the west end of the loft. The crush of women at the door leading to the stairway slammed it closed. The doors in this building opened in rather than out." (http://www.historybuff.com/library/refshirtwaist.html). this could have been avoided if there weren't so many young female workers, and more emergency exits that opened out instead of in. But if you want to look a little deeper into how this might have happened, you might say this was because of the huge number of women laboring in the building.According to Brittanica "Much of the tragedy that occurred at the Triangle Shirtwaist Company could have been avoided, but a series of problems made survival near impossible for many trapped in the building.

Me - Keep your posts on topic, guys. Also, look into the deeper causes and reason the fire was such a tragedy. Val began to touch on it.
Dec 2, 2012

Kiara J. - Also, the most of the people who died in the fire where under aged girls. #ChildLabor
Dec 2, 2012

Evan B. - #Kiara Where is your evidence?
Dec 2, 2012

 Val gets kids pointed not just toward the cause of the flames—which might have caused few if any casualties—but to the dangerous setup of the factory and the extent of the death toll.   Figure 6.7 (continued)

Figure 6.7 (continued)

 Tana A. - This is hard to explain what happened because the articles that I read don't really go into detail how the fire started. In the ILR School website that you had posted, I read that the owners said that the building was fireproof. But after the fire investigators checked and found out that "without fire escapes, and without adequate exits...". There was no escapes and no adequate exits, they also had locked the doors during work hours. Also it said that in the factory there were barrels of oil that could catch on fire and there was barrels blocking the exits. There were many problems that had maybe caused the people to die, a couple of examples are like the door was locked to the stair well, the fire escape collapsed, short ladders only reached to the 6th floor, long wooden tables became obstacles, oily floors spread the fire quickly, fire nets failed to catch the jumpers who didn't want to burn, no sprinkler system, only pails of water, and flammable barrel of oil. The fire was a tragedy because many people had died and most of them were very young working for money. *less...*

Dec 2, 2012

Kiara J. - I disagree with you #Athee. "The women should've quit when the has the chance. Their LIVES could have been saved and they would have gotten paid fairly." This doesn't make sense to me. If you had done your research, you would notice the women continued to work at the factory because they desperately needed the money. Also, you would have realized there were also about 27 men workers. Finally, how would the workers get paid fairly if the quit their job at the factory? If they quit, they would no longer have a job. Please explain and enlighten us all because I'm positive I'm not the only one who is completely lost. *less...*

Dec 3, 2012

Jina P. - I agree with you, Kiara. And just like a lot of people said, it could have been ignited from a cigarette butt that wasn't fully put out. The cigarette could have been thrown into a waste bin that contained cloth scraps,which are flammable. Also, in the website that Ms. Ahmed posted, it said that sweatshops were unsanitary and dangerous. The owner also didn't know how much each worker was paid, or how much workers were hired. The company was very disorganized, and I believe this is one of the reasons the fire started. But even with the fire, less people could have been killed if the exit doors had been opened, and if the ninth floor fire exit had actually led to a safe place for people. *less...*

Dec 3, 2012

 Kids address and sometimes challenge each other's points directly, and with evidence.

Figure 6.7

ONLINE PARTNERSHIPS

Purpose: Making it easy and natural for students to pursue inquiry questions with kids from around the block, and around the world.

Our high-tech teacher colleague Kristin Ziemke recently had a first grader who blogged about using a new kind of software—and within 24 hours had received comments from 41 people in three countries! The amazing Internet allows our students to connect with people around the world. How cool is that? Where contact was once limited to slo-mo pen pal letters, today students can instantly hang (digitally) with peers, dozens or thousands of miles away. To take advantage of this amazing new opportunity, many teachers are setting up classroom partnerships, where students from different schools pair up to undertake research projects and share their findings.

Ninety Chicago kids in two schools recently conducted a joint, web-based inquiry on the topic of bats. Kristin, her sixth-grade teacher colleague Ben Kovacs, and fourth-grade teacher Autumn Laidler from another Chicago school called the National Teachers Academy all wanted to do a collaborative inquiry project using the latest digital tools. Bats were already a hot topic in Chicago media, with reports of a few rabid bats and some ultimately unrelated swarming behavior downtown. Tantalizing. The three teachers decided that kids of all these ages would be interested in bats, so the topic was settled.

In first grade, Kristin Ziemke's kids were already curious about bats. Kristin's collection of the *National Geographic Young Explorer* series offered a great book about featured bats that piqued kids' curiosity. The 6-year-olds started reading about bats in general, which, of course, led to vampire bats, so dangerous and interesting. As the first graders read about bats, they posted their questions on a blog.

© fstop123.

Back in first grade, Kristin read aloud the book *Bat Loves the Night* by Nicola Davies. The first graders took notes and then narrated them into videos. Amanda's video had four of her drawings, with her recorded narration:

> Baby bats cannot fly.
> They hook onto their parents' stomachs, and they go through that way.
> Bats live in houses.

The fourth and sixth graders watched the first graders' videos online and then added their thinking via video to the blog. The fourth graders recounted their process (see Figure 6.8).

We started learning from our 1st grade partners from what they shared about their bat knowledge. We found out they eat insects which is a very important part of our ecosystem. We have been learning about living and non-living things and how they interact in the environment. We found out that bats are very important to the ecosystems they live in. After watching the first grade videos we back channeled both the things we learned from the first graders and the questions we wanted to investigate ourselves. You can see those below.

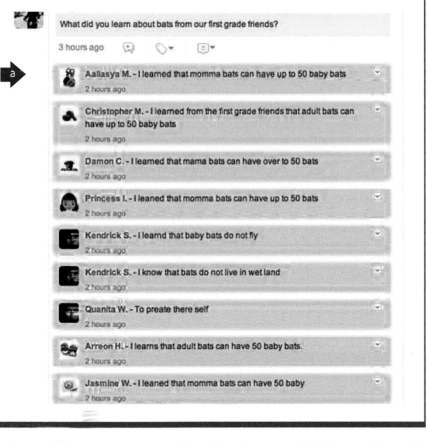

What did you learn about bats from our first grade friends?

3 hours ago

> **Aaliasya M.** - I learned that momma bats can have up to 50 baby bats
> 2 hours ago

> **Christopher M.** - I learned from the first grade friends that adult bats can have up to 50 baby bats
> 2 hours ago

> **Damon C.** - I learned that mama bats can have over to 50 bats
> 2 hours ago

> **Princess I.** - I leaned that momma bats can have up to 50 bats
> 2 hours ago

> **Kendrick S.** - I learnd that baby bats do not fly
> 2 hours ago

> **Kendrick S.** - I know that bats do not live in wet land
> 2 hours ago

> **Quanita W.** - To preate there self
> 2 hours ago

> **Arreon H.** - I learns that adult bats can have 50 baby bats.
> 2 hours ago

> **Jasmine W.** - I leaned that momma bats can have 50 baby
> 2 hours ago

OK, everyone, any questions about how many babies a bat mom can have?

Figure 6.8

Now the kids make another list—of the questions they'd like to investigate about bats.

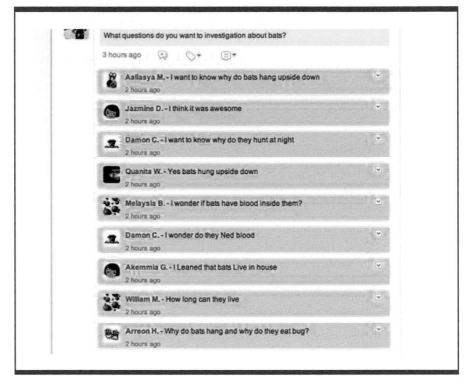

Figure 6.9

All three classes continued with the inquiry over a couple of weeks. The older students were especially fascinated when they discovered in South America the species was preying on livestock and destroying record numbers of cattle.

Finally, all 90 kids then "met" digitally, using the programs TodaysMeet and Google Hangouts. Google Hangouts work much like a Skype call, so from the three classrooms, all the kids could see and hear each other. Todays-Meet allows all participants in a meeting to post comments and questions in a "backchannel"—that way, everyone could join the conversation without needing to speak live to everyone. So there was a huge multimedia sharing of all the things the kids had learned in their inquiries—an online Batfest!

Sixth grader Lena from Ben Kovacs's class summed up the whole experience.

Categories: Blog December 20, 2012 @ 11:04 AM

Vampire Bat Inquiry

Vampire bats lap up blood, they do not suck it. They pierce the skin of animals and let the blood flow, not letting It clot because of the special substance on their tongue. They use echo location which is screeching sounds they make that bounce off objects and come back to them so that they can avoid obstacles and find their predators, this is their only way of getting around in the dark because they have poor eyesight.

This is just some of the information that we the 6th grade class of Burley found when collaborating with Ms. Laidler's 4th grade at NTA and the first grade class downstairs at Burley.

This was a very exciting time for our class, getting to work together through video chats, blog posts and quick chats. So much learning was going on besides learning about vampire bats. We learned how to collaborate with a large amount of people, we learned from the other classes by hearing how they learn and how they respond to projects like these that are exciting. But there was lots of awesome learning about vampire bats to, the process was not super easy for some groups but in the end everything turned out great.

We started out by reading an article on the farmers that want to wipe out the population of bats because they are killing their livestock. After reading the article we started to develop some questions for topics that we wanted to learn about. My topic was what are the symptoms of getting a vampire bat bite, what do you do to stop the infection? Then we got answers to our lingering questions by doing research. We didn't make presentations out of cardboard and art supplies after we found the answers to our questions, but we did get to share our info through a quick chat online with NTA school and the first graders in our building, and then in the same day we video chatted with them and gave more answers to their questions verbally.

This was a great learning process for us, NTA and the Burley first graders. There was lots of team building, and fun!

Figure 6.10

EMAIL AND FAREWELL

Purpose: Using email to build deep relationships with young people.

Very early in our introductory chapter, we talked about how letters—this very personal channel of communication—can help teachers build strong and close relationships with students. We return to that thought now as we come to the end of the book.

One of Elaine's extraordinary students, Red Horse BlackElk-Jim, did some beautiful writing in her class, sharing reflections on his childhood growing up on a pueblo here in New Mexico. This piece was written in one draft, during class.

Friendship

By RedHorse BlackElk-Jim

I first met my friend Monty Wallace August, 1997 in Ganado Elementary; it was Kindergarten and my first day of school. I was scared and not sure what to expect of this new place. Just so happen on the bus ride home I sat next to Monty, and I told him my clan and where I was from, who was my grandfather. Over the years we discovered our grandfathers served together in World War II. As time went on we continued to grow a stronger bond than just friends, we became brothers.

From then on we always had the same classroom, and when school would let out for Thanksgiving we always went hunting. Our grandfathers showed us how to look for deer tracks and how to set up in a tree to await a young buck. I recall a time, it was the fall of 2002 and we decided to leave earlier than the usual 7 a.m. and go further north of our usual trail. It was cold that morning and our breath could be seen in the light of the four-wheeler. I clenched and squeezed my eye sight through low branches that hugged the morning dawn. We must have driven for an hour and finally come to a clearing. The morning sun was just peeking over the tree tops and the mist was ascending from the tall wet grass, frost still hung from the tips. I pushed the four-wheeler into the trees and trailed my brother about 3 seconds behind him. Climbing over fallen trees, looking at the grass to see if there had been any tracks from the night before.

It was almost noon and I heard branches snapping from across the clearing. Peering through the binoculars, I saw a young buck brushing his horns against the tree, and I whistled lightly to Monty and pointed across the clearing. He smiled and locked an arrow on his bow, slowly crept towards me and told me, "If we walk more further west we can be down wind and you can flank him as he runs

---

Figure 6.11 (continued)

Figure 6.11 (continued)

past you." I nodded and we walked away with the adrenalin tickling up my chest and down my arms. Placing each foot like a secret and stopping to see if the young buck was still there, I looked through the binoculars one more time and saw that the buck was eating and only 50 yards away, but there was no cover unless I crawled across the ground and mounted myself on the edge of the hill. Gently I laid on the ground and felt the cold ground soak through my jacket and grate my skin. I could hear Monty's deer call, but I wasn't ready.

The young buck stuck up his head and looked around. I felt like his eyes were the spotlight of the watch tower, the eye of Mordor in Lord of the Rings. I picked up the pace lightly and rolled along the side of the hill and locked my arrow knock in the string. A reflection glistened across my bow and I could see my father's designs. I brought back the memory of when my father made bows for my brother and I. He didn't want us hunting with rifles.

I heard rustling in the pine needles and I recognized Monty's alert, the buck would be coming now. I inhaled a breath and pulled back the arrow and waited for the buck to dart by. And so did the buck dart by, leaping several feet in the air, and timing his jumps, I finally releasing the arrow, the string snapping my wrist. The arrow glided straight and pierced the buck in the rib and landed sideways. I loaded a second arrow quickly and walked over to where our trophy landed. "He down," Monty said as he walked up behind me and knelt down to check for a pulse. He smiled and shook my hand. I could feel the cold palm meet my sweaty palm.

"For once we have something to trophy around at the house." I laughed and I took tobacco out from my pouch and we whispered our prayers together. Giving thanks to the sun and the deer itself and told the deer how we didn't hunt for sport, but to feed our family. We stood up and brushed our knees and grabbed the buck, slowly waddling back to the four-wheeler.

That was an amazing hunting trip I took with my brother. At school we would joke around about how big the deer was and showed off pictures of us smiling standing next to our kill. I look at the picture of us both holding one side of the antlers, dirt across our faces. We have been brothers for seventeen years and still counting.

Figure 6.11

We've always thought it strange that teachers routinely respond to the gift of student writing with red marks instead of words.

In this time of relentless reform, rampant standardization, and proliferating tests, a wedge is being driven between us and our students. As public education becomes more adversarial and more polarized, as our pay is more closely harnessed to students' scores on tests of no validity, we are being positioned to treat kids as just another obstacle or problem, even as opponents.

There's only one way out of this trap; we must recommit to our students as people and to our work as a calling. Students are not data, and neither are we. Using letters in our teaching is not just a practical way to enhance student understanding of the curriculum, thought it does that job magnificently well. When we fully commit to one-to-one writing, we can make our teaching space a sacred place. Young people can connect to each other, and we to them, not just as students and educators, but as friends, as souls, as kindred spirits. That enchanting human connection has always been the supreme reward of the teaching life.

Look what we get, if we give.

From: RedHorse BlackElk-Jim <redhorse.blackelkjim@email.sfcc.edu>

To: askelaine <askelaine@aol.com>

Sent: Sun, Dec 9, 2012 8:05 pm

Dear Mrs Daniels,

I wanted to thank you for all the encouragement you have given to the class this past semester. In this class I had expected more book lessons in English, but no, instead our assignments were responses. The assignments reopened a part of me that I thought had been asleep for too long.

All of the responses to the stories in the brown book, became stepping stones in my life to closing chapters I was afraid to talk about. At times when I wrote the papers for your class I found myself back in my old room. I saw myself scribbling in my journals again, digging up the past buried in my backyard and carrying it to the bridge. Standing there on the bridge and dropping the past into the water.

Before I took your class, I had given up on writing entirely. I felt that this gift, this art had no more meaning in my life. All of the dark days were over, but no they weren't at all. Now I'm writing again and seriously thinking about writing stories again.

The last story we read called Angry Fathers, I felt I closed something off I had with another person. A passed relationship I wasn't planning on letting go of. Then I saw it from a different perspective and only wished for the best for the future. Even the best part, when I had come back from burying my uncle in October. I wanted to run away and say, "screw the world." I knew I had to finish what I started, because that's what my uncle would have wanted me to do. I wrote this journal entry when I was going to Gallup from Farmington:

Figure 6.12 (continued)

Figure 6.12 (continued)

Its flat and a few hills make the road bounce and turn. I was by myself and had oldies playing like Creedence Clearwater Revival, Bob Dylan, and Motley Crue. I was singing along to 'Switch Hitchhiker." I remembered the photos my uncle took when he use to go riding on his motorcycle. So I imagined myself on the back of a motorcycle and the wind howling around the roar of the bike. Ahead I see this black dot bouncing over the road as it got closer. The shape of the figure is a motorcycle and time stopped for a quick second. I looked over at the biker and saw my uncle. The sun lit up his mustache, his facial expression was still and he nodded his head at me. Then he put his left hand down to wave the peace sign. Then the air came swarming in like locusts around my ears. I looked back in my side view mirror and saw it was another person riding his bike.

From that moment on I knew it was going to be hard, but I had to hold on in life and enjoy the ride.

Thank you again,

Red

Dear Red Horse,

I just got back from Denver visiting my husband's sister who has Alzheimer's. Ahh, such sorrow. At the same time, she is so loving and happy seeming. She tells us she loves us every minute along with often misplaced kisses. She loves everyone right now. How strange life can be that she brings such positive energy to people despite the crevasses in her brain.

To come back to your beautiful letter, it has affected me very deeply. I knew right off that you had a depth and insight that was unique. From my first sight of your writing, I knew that you had so much so say. Your culture tears at you sometimes, as much as it gives you your strength. You write with poetry in your heart. I think you have some anger to drop off that bridge. I've learned so much from what you've written. As an observer of life, you see it from your own distinctive vantage point.

I feel so sad about your losing your uncle. The way you describe him on his motorcycle reminds me of Alexie's description of Eugene in *The Absolutely True Story of a Part Time Indian*. There's a cartoon that I love of him on his bike.

Our Christmas tree this year is festooned with ornaments from my sister Alison who died almost 2 years ago. I keep wanting to call her. We used to talk every day. In my dreams I pick up the phone and she's there. She's usually telling me what to do, but boy, do I miss her.

The brown book is heavy duty. I'm so glad you could make so many connections and even change your path because of that one story. I really like the stories. I guess I often choose to read heavy stuff. I did have one student tell me she was glad the class was over because the stories were so upsetting! She's at a tender time in her life.

Thank you, Red Horse, for your very kind words. A teacher can wait a long time to have someone reach back in the way that you have. It means more than you know. Hang in there at Target over the holidays. I would be so pleased if you'd stay in touch. I'll always be happy to read any writing you choose to share.

Sincerely,

Elaine

Figure 6.12

MANAGEMENT TIPS FOR DIGITAL DISCUSSIONS

Tablets. Students can have brisk and focused written conversations on a wide variety of devices if (and this is a BIG if) everyone has the same kind of device and knows how to use it fluently, without any technological friction slowing down the process. Students can physically pass around their tablets and have a written conversation just like on paper, typing instead of writing their comments—if everyone's got the same program running and the same skills to use it.

Cell Phones. It's unfortunate that schools are still trying to criminalize kids' cell phones, when they can be such a helpful (and free) learning tool. If your school allows cell phones for academic purposes in class (quick research, phone interviews of experts, texted discussions with other students, etc.), lucky you! Every single kid doesn't have to have a phone; you can form pairs or small groups around the kids who do.

Group Size. While digital technologies allow for interaction in pairs or small groups, very often we end up with larger audiences when we get techy. Nothing wrong with that—how cool that today's students can potentially reach out to the whole world. But the dynamic also shifts when we have more whole-class and whole-world discussions. It's easier for reticent or unmotivated kids to check out, bypass, or slide by. So we recommend that you frequently use the capacity of most blog programs to put kids into several smaller "rooms" where there is higher social pressure to participate.

School-Appropriate Language. Since our humble classroom communications may now flash throughout the known world in a nanosecond, and live on the web forever, we need to be extra careful in teaching school-appropriate language and guarding against bullying behavior. We prefer doing T-chart lessons where we co-create the rules with kids, so they buy into mutually developed constraints. One good suggestion from a fifth grader: "If you wouldn't say it to your mother, don't say it on the computer."

The Teacher's Role. With handwritten conversations, we monitor kids' work by wandering the room, looking over shoulders. When the discussions go digital, we shift to virtual supervision, looking in on kids' work from our computer. And we coach actively. In the Triangle Shirtwaist discussion on pages 210–212, Sara Ahmed jumps right into the kid-kid conversation to say things like "Be careful, this is not a simple answer. Use evidence in your responses and push each other's thinking" and "Keep your posts on topic, guys. Also, look into the deeper causes and reason the fire was such a tragedy."

R U kewl w/ textspeak? Teachers differ on whether to allow "textspeak" abbreviations, icons, and symbols in online discussions. We're permissive on that question. Kids can speak and write in a wide range of dialects, while still shifting to Standard English when the occasion calls for it. And if we want engaged discussion, why rule out tools that make this extra fun and real for kids?

Participation Quotas. From time immemorial, teachers have been trying to set minimum participation levels for discussions, writing assignments, and almost any other school activity. With these digital discussions, we hope that there will be so much intrinsic interest in our good assignments and the joy of the technology that we won't have to bribe/threaten students with points. Bottom line: It's fine to set a minimum number of posts or lines filled per student, per conversation. We keep points to "all or nothing," 10 or zero. Use the notes in class to spark discussion or writing; but don't spend your weekend trying to tell a 6-point note from a 7-point note. And we never grade these notes for grammar, spelling, or mechanics because students have been given no time to revise and edit them, nor is that the aim of these writing to learn activities.

Works Cited

Allington, Richard. 2012. "Reading, the Core Skill: Every Child, Every Day." *Educational Leadership*. Vol. 69, No 6. March.

Atwell, Nancie. 1987. *In the Middle: Reading and Writing With Adolescents*. Portsmouth, NH: Heinemann.

Britton, James. 1975. *The Development of Writing Abilities, 11–18*. London: Macmillan Education.

Calkins, Lucy McCormick. 1986. *The Art of Teaching Writing*. Portsmouth, NH: Heinemann.

Daniels, Harvey. 2002. *Literature Circles: Voice and Choice in Book Clubs and Reading Groups*. Portland, ME: Stenhouse.

Daniels, Harvey, and Nancy Steineke. 2013. *Texts and Lessons for Teaching Literature*. Portsmouth, NH: Heinemann.

Daniels, Harvey, and Nancy Steineke. 2011. *Texts and Lessons for Content-Area Reading*. Portsmouth, NH: Heinemann.

Daniels, Harvey, and Nancy Steineke. 2006. *Mini-Lessons for Literature Circles*. Portsmouth, NH: Heinemann.

Daniels, Harvey, and Steven Zemelman. 2004. *Subjects Matter: Every Teacher's Guide to Content-Area Reading*. Portsmouth, NH: Heinemann.

Daniels, Harvey, Steven Zemelman, and Nancy Steineke. 2005. *Content-Area Writing: Every Teacher's Guide*. Portsmouth, NH: Heinemann.

Elbow, Peter. 1973. *Writing Without Teachers*. London: Oxford University Press.

Fulwiler, Toby. 1987. *The Journal Book*. Portsmouth, NH: Heinemann.

Fulwiler, Toby. 2000. *The Letter Book: Ideas for Teaching College English*. Portsmouth, NH: Heinemann.

Graves, Donald. 1983. *Writing: Teachers and Children at Work*. Portsmouth, NH: Heinemann.

Harvey, Stephanie, and Anne Goudvis. 2007. *Strategies That Work: Teaching Comprehension for Understanding and Engagement*, 2nd edition. Portland, ME: Stenhouse.

Harvey, Stephanie, Anne Goudvis, Kristin Ziemke, and Katie Muhtaris. 2013. *Connecting Comprehension and Technology*. Portsmouth, NH: Heinemann FirstHand.

Ivey, Gay, and Joan Broaddus. 2007. "A Formative Experiment Investigating Literacy Engagement Among Adolescent Latina/o Students Just Beginning to Read, Write, and

Speak English." *Reading Research Quarterly.* Vol. 42, No. 4. October/November/December. Pp. 512–545.

Kajder, Sara. 2010. *Adolescents and Digital Literacies: Learning Alongside Our Students.* York, ME: Stenhouse.

National Governors Association Center for Best Practices and the Council of Chief State School Officers. 2010. *Common Core State Standards for English Language Arts & Literacy in History/Social Studies, Science, and Technical Subjects.* Retrieved from www.corestandards .org/assets/CCSSI_ELA%20Standards.pdf

Northeast Foundation for Children. 2013. *Responsive Classroom.* Retrieved from www .responsiveclassroom.com

Ontario Ministry of the Attorney General. 2004. *Public Safety Related to Dogs Statute Law Amendment Act, 2004.* Retrieved from http://www.attorneygeneral.jus.gov.on.ca/english/ news/2004/20041026-pitbulls-bg.asp

Routman, Regie. 2004. *Writing Essentials.* Portsmouth, NH: Heinemann.

Staton, Jana. 1985. *Dialogue Journals With Students With Special Needs.* Washington, DC: Center for Applied Linguistics.

Zemelman, Steven, Harvey Daniels, and Arthur Hyde. 2012. *Best Practice: Bringing Standards to Life in America's Classrooms*, 4th edition. Portsmouth, NH: Heinemann.

Index

CORWIN

A SAGE Company

The Corwin logo—a raven striding across an open book—represents the union of courage and learning. Corwin is committed to improving education for all learners by publishing books and other professional development resources for those serving the field of PreK–12 education. By providing practical, hands-on materials, Corwin continues to carry out the promise of its motto: **"Helping Educators Do Their Work Better."**